How to Have a Soul Winning Church

By
GENE EDWARDS

Rusthoi
Soul Winning Publications
Montrose, California

MCMLXII

SOUL WINNING PUBLICATIONS
TYLER, TEXAS

Copyright assigned to

GOSPEL PUBLISHING HOUSE
SPRINGFIELD, MISSOURI

MCMLXIII

CONTENTS

TO HELEN

The Divinely chosen companion of my life
The reality of my fondest dreams
The reflector of her Savior's image
And my eternal sweetheart

INTRODUCTION

THE PURPOSE OF THE BOOK

This book is for Christians whose hearts are on fire. This is for the visionary, the idealist. It is for the man who is not satisfied with the *status quo* in Christianity, and who believes that there is something big that can be done about it. This is for the Christian who believes the church and its people can be everything He wanted them to be—to fulfill the purpose for which he ordained them. This is for the spiritual optimist in a dark age.

This book was *not* written for the church with a 26-hour-a-day, eight-day-a-week program of activities that wants to sandwich into its crammed schedule, a program of evangelism. Nor is it written for the church that might have a goal to win "50 people to Christ" or "100 people to Christ" this year. This book may help you, and it may even revolutionize your church program. But it was not written with you in mind.

This book is for the minister who desires to have the most effective Christian witnesses and soul winning church possible—for the church that wants to see men coming to Christ *every* week.

The goal of this book is to show you how a church can witness to, and seek to win, every human being in the city. This book is for the Christian who, more than anything else in all the world, wants to be a soul winner.

This is for the minister who wants to grow laymen in his church, who do nothing but talk soul winning, eat soul winning, dream soul winning, and do soul winning.

Let us add, though, that no matter how revolutionary an idea is, it will not work if it is not put into action! This is a revolutionary day we live in. It calls for revolutionary ideas and methods. The pastor or Christian worker who picks up this book must not just *want* to win souls. He must *win* souls. He will have to lead his people up and out, into a great new sphere of Christian achievement.

This book is written for thousands who believe the Church — in this dark hour — can still turn the tide of history and become the assassin of Communism and the redeemer of society.

This book is written for men who want to win the world to Christ.

PART I

THE CASE FOR
PERSONAL EVANGELISM

CHAPTER 1

A BRIEF HISTORY OF EVANGELISM

It would be interesting to pay a visit to a church of the 1st century, and study their program of evangelism. They could quickly tell us how to have a soul winning church. If we could make such a journey back to those churches, we would probably be amazed at our discoveries.

Stopping off at the Church of Ephesus, our visit might begin something like this.

"Good evening, Aquila! We understand you're a member of the church here. Could we come in and visit a while?"

"Certainly, come in."

"If you don't mind, we would like for you to tell us about the way the churches here in Asia Minor carry on their evangelistic program. We read that you have been a member of a church in Corinth and Rome, as well as now, the one here in Ephesus. So you should be very well qualified to tell us about evangelism in a New Testament church. If you don't mind, we'd also like to visit the church while we're here."

"Sit down. And as for as that goes, you're already in the church. It meets in my home."

"You don't have a church building?"

"What's a church building? No, I guess we don't."

"Tell me, Aquilla, what is your church doing to evangelize Ephesus? What are you doing to reach the city with the Gospel?"

"Oh, we've already evangelized Ephesus. Every person in the city clearly understands the Gospel."

"What?!!"

"Yes . . . is that unusual?"

"How did the church do it? You certainly don't have any radios or televisions. Did you have a lot of evangelistic campaigns?"

"No. As you have probably heard, we tried mass

meetings in this area, but most of the time we would end up in jail!"

"Then how?"

"Oh, don't you know? We just visited every home in the city. That's the way the church in Jerusalem first evangelized that city.* The disciples there evangelized the entire city of Jerusalem in a very short time. All the other churches in Asia Minor have followed that example."

"Is it effective everywhere?"

"Yes, it is. There are so many converts that some of the pagan religious leaders fear their own religions will die. When Brother Paul left Ephesus for the last time, he reminded us to keep on following this same procedure."†

"Aquila, this is amazing! Why, at this rate, there is no telling how many people are going to hear the Gospel and respond."

"Oh, haven't you heard? We've already taken the Gospel to every person in Asia Minor — both Jews and Greeks."**

"Why, that's impossible. You don't mean *everyone!*"

"Yes, everyone."

"But that would include Damascus, Ephesus, dozens of large cities. And then towns and villages — and what about the nomadic tribes on the desert? How long did it take the churches to reach all these people?"

"Not long — 24 months to be exact.** The same thing is happening in North Africa and Southern Europe. The Gospel has reached Spain too. We've heard of a land called England, and several Christians may have reached there. We hope to have fulfilled the Great Commission of Jesus by the close of the century."

---

* Acts 5:42
† Acts 20:20
** Acts 19:10

"Aquila, what you're telling us is incredible. You have done more in a generation than we have done in a thousand years."

"That's strange. It's been rather simple for us to do. It's hard to realize things have moved so slowly for you. Maybe you're going at it in the wrong way."

THE DEATH AND REBIRTH OF EVANGELISM

How did 1st century Christianity do so much in evangelism? Why has 20th century Christianity done so little in comparison?

After 1900 years—we have not yet rediscovered the way to perform such remarkable accomplishments. We would do well to recall why the situation exists as it does.

The Death of Evangelism

In the 2nd century, Christianity became entangled in theological controversy. The 3rd century saw a strong growth of apostasy. The 4th century made the apostasy complete. Christianity was then plunged into 1,000 years of darkness.

This 1,000 years is what completely separates us from any direct contact with New Testament Christianity. We often fail to remember this fact, and sometimes feel that our present day methods are all New Testament in origin. A close examination of the New Testament, and a historical study of the origin of our present day methods, quickly dispel this idea.

The Reformation

Under the leadership of Martin Luther, Christianity began to move out of this 1,000 years of darkness. But the Reformation of the 15- and 1600's was limited in its scope. This was primarily a theological reformation—a return to the examination of the Word of God.

Many Things Left Unsettled

The writings of Luther drew the battle lines of the Reformation. The subjects he wrote about and discussed pretty well set the boundaries of Biblical exploration for a very long time. But Luther left many aspects of Christianity untouched.

For instance, he said little about eschatology. It was 300 years after Luther before this subject came under prominent study.

He said little or nothing about missions, and the evangelization of the world. It was left to William Carey, in the 1790's, to bring this New Testament concept back to the forefront.

The Holy Spirit received little attention in the Reformation. It has been only in this century that the doctrine and the place of the Holy Spirit has found worthy consideration.

The period since the Reformation has been a "groping back" to New Testament concepts. We have not yet bridged the gap. There are many New Testament ideas, concepts and doctrines that we have yet to rediscover.

The Rise of Traditional Concepts

Most of the programs, ideas, terminology, and organizations that we have in our churches today have evolved through tradition, and have no real, clear cut New Testament basis for their existence.

For instance, it is usually shocking, and often very humorous, when we realize that the *church building* falls in this category. The Reformation leaders took the idea of the church building from the Catholics, without thought. But the church building is a 3rd century idea, and has no New Testament precedent.

Even such sacred terms as "the pulpit", "missionary", and "Sunday School", have no clear cut Biblical origin.

The list is endless.

THE ORIGIN OF MODERN EVANGELISM

In the New Testament, there were *two* very definite, predominant types of evangelization—mass evangelism, and personal evangelism.

By the 3rd century, both were very largely lost. Nor was there any significant revival of evangelism during the Reformation. Incredible as it seems, there was no significant return to evangelism until *just* 200 years ago. At that time, *one* kind of New Testament evangelism made its reappearance. It made its first strong re-entrance after a 1600 year absence, through the ministry of John Wesley. We can be thankful that he gave back to us the concept of *mass* evangelism.

Unfortunately, the other form of New Testament evangelism has not yet made its re-entry into Christian history. It waits in the wing, perhaps hoping soon to command the center of the stage once more. We can only guess how dramatic the entrance will be. Mass evangelism made a dramatic reappearance with John Wesley. Perhaps we can hope for as much again!

What About Personal Evangelism?

Personal evangelism is talked about. People write books about it. Men preach fervent messages about the need of it. And in isolated cases, you find a few people who do it.

But no great, sweeping return to personal evangelism has come. There has not been a time in the last 1800 years, when a great movement of personal witnessing has gripped a large portion of Christian people. Open your history books and turn back through nearly two milleniums. You will discover not even a mention. After 1800 years, the church has not repossessed personal evangelism. It lies, until this very hour, in a musty stack, labeled: "Undiscovered Truths of the New Testament".

What has been the end result of going this long without a vibrant repossession of such a cardinal truth? Is it nothing really? It is just that the most powerful and necessary concept of Christianity is still dead! Just that we have a car without a motor; a plane without wings; a message—*the Message*—and no *really* efficient way to get it out to the whole world.

A revival—a rediscovery—of personal evangelism will, in truth, be the rediscovery of the spirit of New Testament Christianity.

The Evolution Of Mass Evangelism

Before we trace the origin of other kinds of evangelism that have arisen, let's go back a moment and trace the evolution of "mass evangelism" for the 200 years since its rediscovery.

Under men like George Whitfield, America was introduced to mass evangelism. It found fertile soil in this frontier country. Actually, mass evangelism has gone through several "slumps" and "revivals" since that time. There have been about four high points in the history of mass evangelism. One under Wesley, another under Finney, then Moody, and in our own day, through the God-impelled leadership of Billy Graham.

In the middle 1700's, there came the "camp meeting". Later, in the 1800's, there developed the "protracted meeting" and the "brush arbor". In the late 1800's, when there was a revived interest in mass evangelism, the term which was often used was "revival". The terms "revival" and "mass evangelism" began to get intertwined in our thinking, as well as in our terminology. Today, we have the very highly organized "evangelistic campaign", either church-centered or city wide.

There are certain unalterable spiritual principles in mass evangelism that are eternal, and that do not change. These laws have come to be recognized and understood in our day. Consequently mass evangelism has become a highly organized and exacting science. There is what might be called a spiritual "science of mass evangelism".

Though often still neglected by many, mass evangelism today is the greatest single New Testament method of evangelism we employ, and an oft used instrument of God to the salvation of multitudes.

The Origin And Evolution Of "Enlistment Evangelism"

Mass evangelism does have certain limitations. Because it does—and because personal evangelism has lain dormant so long—other kinds of evangelism were sure to be invented to fill in the gap.

Such is the case of *"Enlistment Evangelism"*.

As Christianity developed and spread in America, it began to follow the lines of development of the church in Europe. Christianity became more "church building" centered; it moved almost all its sphere of activity inside the local church building.

Out of this, in the later years of the 1800's, came the birth of "enlistment evangelism".

Here is how enlistment evangelism began:

It was discovered that by enlisting young boys and girls in Bible school, and by teaching them the Word of God, many would turn to Christ. This is natural. By exposing young hearts to the Gospel, through Bible study, many will naturally respond to Him.

As this method began producing results among children, it was expanded to adults. There are many older Christians today who can recall that teaching adults in Bible School is a relatively new idea.

Today, enlistment evangelism, or "educational evangelism", is the most exacting science within the church. More books have been written and more programs and schemes worked out in this field than all other forms of evangelism.

Today, enlistment evangelism is filling in the gap because of our lack of personal soul winning. Probably enlistment evangelism is responsible for more conversions than everything else we do in evangelism combined. Many (perhaps most) denominations depend almost wholly on enlistment evangelism for sustenance and growth.

No doubt, enlistment evangelism has made the greatest contribution to the winning of souls in all of recent history.

We need to keep in mind, though, that this kind of evangelism is only about 100 years old and would probably never have come into existence had the church repossessed a powerful witness for personal soul winning.

Other Forms Of Evangelism

In our technical age, we have seen an amazing array of other kinds of evangelism develop. There have been: motion picture evangelism; evangelism through drama; cartoon evangelism; (these are all audio-visual evangelism). There has been the development of radio and TV evangelism; also literature evangelism; and phonograph records are now employed for evangelism.

In the last decade, we have seen the specialization of evangelism—that is, organizations formed to meet the need of one particularly neglected area, such as: youth evangelism; campus evangelism; evangelism for the Navy, Army, Air Force; migrants; factory workers; etc. Most of these organizations simply employ the conventional methods of 20th century evangelism, with adaptations for their particular group.

A DEFINITION OF TERMS

There are a great number of terms used to describe each type of evangelism. We need some clarity of thought.

Mass evangelism is often referred to in these terms: "revivals" and "evangelistic campaigns".

"Personal evangelism" and "enlistment evangelism" get intertwined with each other in many terms: educational evangelism; visitation evangelism; house to house evangelism; Sunday School evangelism; witnessing; soul winning; etc.

The greatest confusion probably revolves around the term "visitation evangelism". The term is actually ambiguous. In the strictest sense of the word, there is no such thing as visitation evangelism. Personal evangelism is one person talking to another person about his need of Jesus, with the view of bringing him to a decision. A Christian may do personal soul winning by going visiting, but he may also do it in a factory, in his own home, or anywhere on earth.

Enlistment evangelism is the attempt to get an unconverted person enrolled in and under the teaching of the Word of God. Enlistment evangelism also employs visitation, but in no way could enlistment evangelism ever be called soul winning. It is usually nothing more than a visit or call inviting someone to attend and enroll in a class of Bible study.

So there is enlistment evangelism, which is done through visiting. There is also personal soul winning, which is often done through visitation, but can be done anywhere. Personal evangelism, therefore, should not be called visitation evangelism.

Only Two Kinds Of Evangelism

There are really only two kinds of evangelism:

PERSONAL EVANGELISM

and

*IM*PERSONAL EVANGELISM.

Every kind of evangelism is "impersonal evangelism" except, of course, personal evangelism!

Preaching is impersonal. All mass evangelism is. Film, literature, radio, television—all these are completely impersonal, to both the speaker and the hearer. Enlistment evangelism—abstract relation of teacher to pupils—is also impersonal.

This simply means that virtually all the evangelism being done in America has no *personal* quality. There is no individual contact. And yet, Christianity is personal!

17

Evangelism must become personal. How can you prove your love while standing in a pulpit "preaching at" a man sitting 30 yards away! How can any of us really hope to have the most effective proof of Christianity—the proof of a real burden, love, and of personal peace—unless we convey it *person to person*?

The lost man has to take, by faith, that the preacher or teacher really has love, joy and peace. But if that Christian knocks on his door, comes into his home, and pours out his heart, person to person, then he can see and feel the Christian's unique life. His love, joy and peace are all being demonstrated. Preaching then becomes practicing.

We talk about all the wonders of being a Christian. We leave ourselves wide open for some serious doubts on the part of the non-Christian. For he always sees and hears the Gospel as a very abstract, impersonal relationship. He has every right to ask: "If it's so great, why not a little more of the personal touch from His disciples?"

Come down out of the abstract in evangelism! Personal evangelism alone can prove the real heart and worth of the Gospel.

We have had 1800 years of impersonal evangelism. Well enough. It has proven its worth. It's time we reintroduced, on a massive, world-wide scale, the very expression and only proof that the Gospel we preach is true . . . evangelism on the *personal* level!

CHAPTER 2

THE LIMITATIONS OF MASS EVANGELISM

There is only one thing wrong with mass evangelism: there isn't enough of it! This chapter is not to point out problems in mass evangelism, because we desperately need more of it, but it is to set down its limitations.

1. Mass evangelism cannot win the world to Christ.

The first and greatest test to put to any concept in evangelism is this: can it evangelize the whole world? Mass evangelism cannot. There are only a limited number of people who will actually get up, get out of their home, and go hear a preacher. Unless we can find a way to get *everyone* in the world to deliberately go hear a message then it will be impossible for mass evangelism to evangelize the world.

2. Mass evangelism is limited in its ability to get the Gospel across in the clearest possible way!

Any minister can testify of having stood in the pulpit and said over and over, "salvation is free . . . living a good life won't save you . . . you can't work your way to heaven, it's a gift . . ." only to leave the pulpit and ask a non-Christian who was in the audience, why he did not respond to Christ; and receive this reply, "Oh, I don't need it; I live a good life!"

It's still hard to get your message across to someone "30 yards away"! Especially when he is but one person, hidden in a vast crowd of people.

Something artificial and intangibly abstract happens whenever any minister mounts a pulpit. Immediately the listener moves into an unreal world. Often, as you know, a large portion of the audience unconsciously shift their minds into "neutral".

A pastor on the West Coast tells of meeting a young boy in the lobby of the sanctuary, right after the morning service. After talking with the boy, he discovered that he had attended there faithfully for several years. The pastor, somehow, had not met the young man. Inquiring if he were a Christian, the boy said "no", explaining that he wanted to be, but did not know how to become a Christian. The pastor was amazed that even though he had attended that church regularly for years, the boy knew nothing about salvation. Yet it was true. The pastor sat down beside the boy, and explained a few Scriptures. In a moment the boy received Christ into his life.

Daws Trotman, founder of the Navigators, spoke in churches all across the West Coast, presenting this proposition: "If you can tell me five statements or points your pastor has made in the last year, I'll give you ten dollars." Unbelievable? He had many to try, but no takers!

Like it or not our sermons are often never heard by those in the audience, and shortly remembered by those who do listen.

3. It is impersonal.

As has been stated already, mass evangelism can never convey the warmth and love, joy and peace, and the concern, that a personal encounter can do. All of these are so necessary to really convey the riches of Christ Jesus.

4. The results of mass evangelism cannot be sustained.

Mass evangelism must, by its nature, be sporadic. The numerical average cannot be sustained. An evangelistic campaign must, of necessity, have a date set to terminate the effort. For this reason, we have come to accept, as being natural and necessary, a need for having great outpourings of the Holy Spirit, and great ingatherings of souls . . . "twice a year" when the church goes into a crusade.

Pastors of the Southland often testify to having been pastor of rural churches where "you could be converted only in the third week in August . . . because that's when they always schedule their revival meetings."

The results of this tradition are myriad. To the world, it shows the shallowness of our thinking. How many of the unconverted have confided, "Those folks at the church only get concerned about me three weeks before a revival meeting."

Such sporadic times of "refreshing" and "revival" have also left us with a "roller coaster" Christianity—up one day and down the next. It wasn't intended that way, you know ?!

This is not so much the fault of mass evangelism as it is the fact that we have no way of sustaining evangelism, and sustaining the spirit of revival. This can come only when there is a consistent, week-in and week-out, conversion of souls. This, mass evangelism cannot do.

We have not rediscovered the secret of the 1st century church, when it could report:

"And the Lord added to the church . . . *daily*"!

5. The individual Christian cannot participate.

Mass evangelism makes for "spectator Christianity". There is really nothing to do but sit and listen. The individual Christian has little opportunity to be used as an instrument of the Holy Spirit . . . and is thereby cut off from any real growth in Christ. About all he can do in the midst of a tidal wave of revival is "listen to the evangelist." That's not very much. Certainly not enough to sustain the revival when the evangelist leaves.

Mass evangelism cannot resolve the Scriptural command given to laymen to be *"doers* of the Word and not *hearers* only".

One other word might be added about mass evangelism. It has a definite tendency to fade into general disuse after a period of time. Since mass evangelism was rediscovered under John Wesley, there have been several slumps and resurgences in its use.

A great, sweeping revival of the church has usually accompanied a return of mass evangelism. For this reason, we unconsciously associate "revival" and mass evangelism. We have somehow come to reason that "revival" can come only through mass evangelism. All of our "starry eyed" thinking about "Revival" has always been associated with the preaching of the Word. Keep in mind, please, that we have never—*never*—seen a sweep of Personal Evangelism. Not in 1800 years. It is possible that Personal Evangelism could *also* be used as an instrument for ushering in "revival"; just as much as mass evangelism has ever since it was brought back into use 200 years ago.

God may have a greater, more powerful instrument for ushering in revival, that we have never before considered —and certainly have never experienced.

CHAPTER 3

THE DRAWBACKS OF ENLISTMENT EVANGELISM

Enlistment evangelism holds a strong position of acceptance today. Its influence and its defenders are many. For some people, devotion to this idea is used as a measure of denominational loyalty. It is commonplace to hear, in virtually every great religious convention, such statements as these:

(the author has personally noted these following)

"Enlistment evangelism is the greatest single contribution to evangelism in the 20th century."

"It is the best way to win souls."

"I defy any man to show me a better way to win souls."

There is no doubt that enlistment evangelism stands today as the greatest single factor in the conversion of the largest number of souls . . . today. But what if . . . just by chance, what if . . . a better way exists? Any man-made method that is regarded as this *perfect* can bear a little inspection! Some questions are in order:

Can enlistment evangelism bring about the evangelization of an entire community?

Can it bring about the evangelization of the entire world?

Just how large a portion of the people can enlistment evangelism actually reach?

How large a percentage of people will enlistment evangelism *not* work on?

If it is the greatest method of 20th century evangelism, then what has 20th century evangelism accomplished?

Does the mammoth emphasis that enlistment evangelism receives in time, energy, and organization, justify the final results?

Does it do any harm, with all the good it accomplishes?

THE RESULTS OF ENLISTMENT EVANGELISM

First, here are some statistics on enlistment evangelism, as presented by several of the best authorities in the field. Please study them *very* carefully.

> Evangelical churches average winning 1 out of 5 unsaved persons that they enlist*
>
> The church wins only one out of 240 unsaved people in the community who are *not* enlisted.
>
> Eighty per cent of all converts today are won through enlistment evangelism. Only 20 per cent are won in all other ways.
>
> BUT:
> Eighty per cent of all those who are enlisted still pass through *without* ever being converted!

To these statistics, we must also add two more:

> Ninety per cent of the American people almost *never* attend church.
>
> Ninety-seven per cent of all the people you invite to church do *not* accept the invitation.

Recently an outstanding Christian leader put enlistment evangelism in a new light by saying: "It is the greatest substitute for soul winning ever invented."

Let's cast these facts in another light:

Let's say that there are 1,000 lost people in your community. This means 80 to 90% of them almost never go to church. Enlistment Evangelism can *reach* a maximum of 10% of this 1,000 people, which means reaching 100 people. Let's say your church is above average and you

---

* Southern Baptists report they win 1 out of 3 that they enlist in classes. A few others report a little better than 1 out of 5.

24

win 1 out of 3 of these 100 that you enlist. That means you will win about 33.

Enlistment evangelism, at its best, can win only 33 out of 1,000 people! That leaves 900 enlistment evangelism can *not* enlist and 977 it can *not* win!

(Remember too, that the average evangelical church wins 1 out of 5, not 1 out of 3.)

Here is one fact: we fail to win 80 per cent of all people we enlist. This is proof that enlistment evangelism is operating almost completely void of any personal witnessing. We rely almost exclusively on the method itself to produce the results. Hence, we rely on it to serve as a substitute for personal witnessing.

Many valiant efforts have been made to get personal soul winning into the integral framework of enlistment evangelism. But the method always triumphs over the principle. People always revert to urging the lost to become enrolled in a class.

Examine this fact: We win one out of five lost people we enlist. We win only one out of 240 that we do not enlist. Some see this as a statistic to put more emphasis on enlistment evangelism. But what about the other 239? Do you know why they were *not* won? It was *not* because they were not enlisted! It was because they *refused* to be enlisted! This is a glaring fact we have overlooked.

We need to look at that 239 unconverted in a new light. They are in the same category as the 97 out of 100 who do not go to church when invited. These 239 will not respond to enlistment evangelism—or any other kind of evangelism that the church is employing to reach them.

We do not need more emphasis on enlistment evangelism. It already holds nearly 100 per cent of our attention. We need to turn our thoughts to those on whom enlistment evangelism *will not work!*

Have you ever stopped to realize we have *no* program for reaching those who *refuse* to be enlisted!

What is the maximum number of people enlistment evangelism can reach?

One pastor said firmly, "Statistics show we can reach 1 out of 5 people in America with enlistment evangelism. Some churches reach 1 out of 3." No, this is not correct! We *win* 1 out of 5 that are *enlisted*, but we are only able to actually enlist about 10% of a community.

If you could *enlist* 10% of the unconverted people in your community — and could win 1 out of 5 of these — then you would be winning 2% of the unsaved people in your community.

Statistics bear this out. We are winning about two out of every 100 lost people in America with enlistment evangelism. But we are working at the program as if it could win *all* 100 per cent.

Now consider where this leaves a local church. 'You are left with *no* program to reach 98 per cent of the lost people in your community.

Here are some other things to consider as we look at the limitations of enlistment:

1. Enlistment often undermines the work of the Gospel.

Done properly, enlistment evangelism would never have caused this. But because we allowed it to become the complete and universal substitute for winning men to Christ, and because it is *the* great, single emphasis in church evangelism, it has been just that.

The minister stands to preach the Gospel. Over and over he says: "Church membership will not save . . . being baptized cannot get you to heaven . . . going to church does not make you a Christian!"

What happens when the service is over?

Christians pour out of the church building, and wherever they go, they spend the entire week *inviting* the lost to come to Sunday School.

What is the result?

The result is predictable. If you were a lost person and all you ever heard from Christians was, "Come to church" and "Come to Sunday School", what would *you* think a person had to do to become a Christian? There would be only one logical conclusion to draw! We have only ourselves to blame because most of the people in this nation think that by attending a church they will become Christians. This is the only emphasis they hear, because of our disproportionate emphasis on enlistment.

Most visitation done today is *enlistment* visitation. A lost person does not have the spiritual wisdom to understand that when he has been invited a dozen times to enroll in a Sunday School, we are primarily concerned about his relationship to Christ. We are. But he thinks—and has every right to think—that we are concerned only about his relationship to the church.

If ever we are to stop this undermining ourselves, our Lord, the Gospel, and even curtailing the effectiveness of the church building by our over emphasis of it, THEN WE MUST *STOP* INVITING THE LOST TO *CHURCH*. WE MUST *START* INVITING THEM TO *CHRIST!!*

We must learn this immovable New Testament principle of evangelism: "You point a man first to Christ, then to the church." It is *not* the other way around.

2. It is a mechanical process.

Overdependence on enlistment evangelism actually forfeits the office work of the Holy Spirit. We place all of our confidence in a method, and soon lose sight of dependence on Him.

("You take 5 lost people and put them in *here*, turn the crank, and 1 Christian will come out here.")

3. It hardens people to the Gospel.

By overemphasizing class enlistment to a non-Christian, you will actually harden him. When he has said "no" over and over again to efforts to be enrolled, he conditions himself into a negative attitude. If someone should come to speak to him about Jesus, he is already in a negative frame of mind. Even though he may desire to know Jesus as Saviour, years of saying "no" to lesser invitations has often done its work too well!

4. It limits interest in Evangelism.

Every pastor can testify to the frustrating results of trying to enlarge visitation to a great, inclusive program for everyone. There seems to be a mental barrier. Prospect visitation is almost always done by classes. Invariably, there is the insurmountable attitude of "let the teacher do it". The class member looks at himself as a "pupil" only; and therefore neither qualified nor needed in making visits.

And what pastor is there among us that does not have someone who refuses to visit anyone except prospects for *his own* class.

We also face the constant problem of the visitation program degenerating until it becomes nothing but an absentee visitation. The great majority of visitation programs today are exactly that, and nothing else. The teacher constantly checks his records to see who was absent last Sunday. He then goes to make a visit which usually begins, "John, we surely did miss you last Sunday. If you had only been there, we would have had 100 per cent attendance!"

This is *not* evangelism . . . you know!

5. Overemphasis on enlistment evangelism lowers the quality of teachers.

In their zeal to follow to the last degree, the science of enlistment, churches make methods a god, and critical problems crop up. We often hear:

"If we form a new class of ten members,
it will mean two new converts!"

A rush to create a new area of enlistment begins, because "a new class always wins more". We let the class create the teacher. But in the economy of God, quality is more important than quantity. The teacher should create the class. We work on the system: we need a new class, so get a teacher. We should work from this vantage point: we have a very qualified teacher, now we can create a new class!

Our zeal for new classes often causes us to scrape the bottom of the barrel for a new teacher—one who is not qualified, morally, spiritually, or doctrinally. Such teachers are often uninterested, absent or unprepared to teach. We are cast in the roll of beggars, going around hunting for a prospective teacher, imploring him to "make the sacrifice" of being a teacher.

The Word of God abounds in texts warning against letting any except the spiritually mature teach. In a day when the knowledge of God's Word is so desperately needed, such compromise in the teaching of the Word of God is producing some of the most serious problems of modern Christianity.

If enlistment evangelism were the only way, or if it were the *best* way to win souls, such action might be defended. But when there is a better way to win men to Christ, and without all this backwash and "fallout", then such action is inexcusable.

"Behold, a greater than enlistment is here."

6. Enlistment evangelism works primarily with children.

We come now to the area where enlistment evangelism has produced its largest results. A quick examination of the records of any church will show that the overwhelming portion of the results from enlistment evangelism have been children. The great majority of converts are between the ages of nine and 13. The results diminish proportionately, as you move up the age scale. Enlistment has had *some* results with adults ever since it was included for this age group, some fifty years ago. But compared to the effort and emphasis expended to achieve the results, it has been meager.

Recognizing the effectiveness of enlistment evangelism among children, and at the same time recognizing its dramatic limitations, a natural and justifiable position can be found for it within the church's program of evangelism.

As long as we continue to give paramount place to enlistment evangelism, we will *never* see a return to personal evangelism. One is a method; the other is a principle. Personal evangelism cannot play second fiddle to enlistment evangelism and survive. There is a place for enlistment evangelism, but it must become secondary. People must always be invited to church, certainly. We must always seek to enlist the lost into Bible classes where they will come under the teaching of the Word. But we cannot *start* with this method. It must not be the major thrust of the 20th century church. We cannot treat it as though it were the greatest and only method for community and world evangelization.

We must lead out *first* with the Gospel. We must *first* present Jesus Christ—and present Him to all men. Then, and only then, are we justified in moving into "secondary" evangelism. We can begin to think in terms of enlisting them . . . after they have had the Gospel clearly presented.

Had we given as much time and study and research and *practical* training to *personal* evangelism as we have had in *enlistment* evangelism, if we had spent as much money, hired as many people, promoted and pleaded for personal evangelism, we could have perhaps already totally evangelized our communities . . . and methinks . . . perhaps the entire nation.

CHAPTER 4

"CHURCH BUILDING EVANGELISM"

The 20th century has committed its entire program for evangelizing the community and the world to the two concepts, mass evangelism and enlistment evangelism. Both of these concepts have *one* glaring flaw that prevents them from ever becoming *the* instrument for fulfilling the Great Commission. Yet the church has committed its entire efforts to these two ideas, as though they could achieve world evangelization, immediately.

The flaw is this: the only people who can be won to Christ by these two methods are the lost who will come to the church building to receive the message.

Think of it, the only people who can be won to Christ in an evangelistic campaign are the lost people who will deliberately get up, get dressed, go down to the auditorium, and willingly expose themselves to the preaching of the Word. These are the only possible prospects that we can ever hope to win.

The only people who can be reached by enlistment evangelism are those who will get out of bed early on Sunday morning, get dressed, go down to the church building, enroll themselves, and then come back week after week to be exposed to the teaching of the Bible.

There is only one problem: *Most people will not do this!*

The lost world has been trying to tell us something:

"Please be sure your pastor has a Th.D.;
air condition your building; cushion your pews;
invite us to church via radio, TV, phone calls,
letters, church pages, bulletins, newspaper ads,
and personal visits . . .

"AND WE STILL WILL NOT COME!"

In 1950, when the ministry of Billy Graham was just sweeping America, I served as a counsellor in one of those early campaigns. Every night 12,000 people were jam-

31

packed into the colliseum. It looked as though the world had come out to hear him! But one night, on the way to the meeting with a group of Christians we suddenly realized that we were driving past a half million souls who chose *not* to hear Billy Graham.

Actually, there has never been a time in the history of the world when the church had a program or a personality great enough to get the *real* masses to come to it.

God never intended it that way, either!

We have built our whole scheme of world evangelism on the concept that if *they* will just come, *we* will win them. This is not theologically even tenable. Anyone who has ever read the third chapter of Romans can figure out that the world will never deliberately come to the church building to hear the Gospel. It seems like madness to think we ever believed they might, much less build our whole scheme of evangelism on the idea.

The redeemed children of God love the church. But they love it because they are redeemed! We have been transformed. As hard as it is for us to admit it, the world does not . . . never has . . . never will . . . share our opinion of the church. It's hard to realize; nonetheless it is true: the church and the Sunday School have an appeal of absolute zero to lost people! The poorest product on earth to sell a *lost* soul is the church. He could not be less interested.

Now even though the *church's* appeal to a lost man is zero, CHRIST JESUS—when He is correctly presented— has the greatest single appeal to the human heart in this entire universe.

Ask anyone who found Christ as his Savior when he was an adult, what his attitude was when he went to church, before he found Christ. He will tell you he was bored! Christ alone can transform such an attitude.

Every Sunday, we attempt to evangelize the world . . . by evangelizing the church building. We evangelize every class room and every pew. It is the most evangelized acre on earth. The way we work at it, you'd think the building needed converting. We work as though all the lost people on earth were in the building.

Only one problem: the lost are everywhere *except* there! The masses of the unsaved have never been there ... aren't there now ... never will be.

WHERE ARE THE MASSES ON SUNDAY?

Where are the masses at 11:00 on Sunday morning?

They are everywhere . . . except where we are trying to get them. Most of them are lying in bed with the comics scattered all over the room. Or they are eating breakfast; the children are watching TV. They are mowing their lawns; washing their cars; picnicking; hooking the motor boat to the back of their car; swimming; out for a drive; down at the tavern; and, of late, out shopping.

Where *aren't* they? At church!

Look over your audience on Sunday morning. The average church, even the largest, will rarely have over six or seven "known" lost people in the service. For many churches, that would be a large number indeed.

Are we asking too much of lost people to come to church?

Well, let's turn the question around. Do *you* find it hard to get to Sunday School?

Or here's a better way: does your house look like a tornado hit it at 9:30 Sunday morning? Most Christians find it a real test of their Christianity to keep composure while hurrying to the service. Often you hear: "I needed to come to church. By the time I got myself and the family ready, I had lost my religion!"

And remember: you have Jesus! He has redeemed and transformed you. You *want* to go to church.

Rather than ask "Should we expect lost people to come to church" let's turn our question around: "Is it too much to ask Christians to go to the home of a lost man?"

Until now, we have gotten more cooperation out of the

lost than the saints. *Some* lost people will come to *God's* house. We've succeeded in getting far less Christians to go to the homes of the lost. The lost have proven to be more cooperative than we have! Honestly now, who's on more justifiable grounds? Whom does God expect the most of? God never said anything to lost people about going to church that is anywhere near as demanding as His greatest single command to Christians: *"Go ye* into all the world."

As soon as we have gone to the home of every lost person on earth and clearly presented the Gospel to him, then and then only can we be justified in expecting the lost world to return the call!!

We have already said that you can expect to enlist a maximum of 10 per cent of the unsaved into Sunday School. Statistics say one out of five of those will find Christ.

What about mass evangelism?

You can expect to get about ten per cent of the people in your community to come to an evangelistic campaign at one time or other. Of course, only a fraction of these will respond to the invitation to receive Christ.

This means that you have an absolute maximum of only 20 per cent of the people in your community whom you could ever hope to touch with the Gospel. (10 per cent by mass evangelism; 10 per cent by enlistment).

What about the other 80 per cent? What kind of program do we have to reach them? What program do we have to reach the people in America who *refuse* to come to church?

Here is one of the most startling, fantastic, and unbelievable facts in existence. It only highlights how long personal evangelism has remained outside the realm of our thinking:

THERE IS NOT A DENOMINATION
IN AMERICA THAT HAS A PROGRAM TO
REACH THE PEOPLE WHO WILL NOT
COME TO CHURCH!

If they will come to us, we can reach them. If they refuse to come to us, what is our program? Do you realize there is not a denomination in America that has a program for winning them to Christ? And yet — at an absolute minimum — at least 80% of the unconverted people in America just will *not* go to church . . . under any circumstance.

Our whole 20th century program of evangelism is completely church building centered. This is wrong! God never intended it this way at all. God always intended that we go to them. Not for them to come to us.

Both mass evangelism and enlistment have reached their logical maximum. If our present day method could win America, it would have already done it. We have taken our 20th century program of evangelism and wrung it dry. We have streamlined it, we have used the very latest "Madison Ave" technique to get it across. We have stretched it to the breaking point. Anything we do from now on will be refining refinements. Greater quality, more work, new ideas are going to meet a very, very small percentage of increase. God does not expect us to be technical, publicity, promotional, organizational *geniuses* to have a greater effectiveness in evangelism. We can be sure that the program God uses to sweep a community and evangelize the world will be simple . . . something any church can organize, direct, and *do!*

It is not by might, nor by power . . .

PERSONAL EVANGELISM CAN REACH EVERYONE.

Now take a look at personal evangelism. It goes without saying that personal evangelism is the only form of evangelism that can reach every human being in America, and in the world! Those it cannot win, it *can* evangelize. It is the only instrument on earth that can reach "every creature".

The author has witnessed in hundreds of homes in every part of America, and talked to people about Christ in almost every city in North America, and trained and sent out tens of thousands of laymen to win souls in homes. Most of these laymen had never won a soul to Christ before. Many had never gone visiting before; yet they have gone out to win incalculable thousands to Christ, who have, in turn, been brought into the church. On the grounds of this experience, I am convinced that at least 70 per cent of the people in America can be *won* to Christ *in their homes*.

We can win 70 per cent, and evangelize all 100 per cent!

I believe the average layman can and is willing to go and win them. I will qualify this in only one way: if Christian laymen are trained in the right way, to witness with dignity and wisdom, then at least 70 per cent of the lost people in America can be won to Christ in their own living rooms by consistent visiting.

We are playing with marbles; losing on every battlefield; and looking about at defeat on every hand. We could be using cannon balls instead of marbles. We can be on the offensive—and win at that—on every battlefield of the world.

There is a way. It is available to us . . . here . . . now!

CHAPTER 5

A LOOK AT
NEW TESTAMENT EVANGELISM

We have traced the origin of present day methods and evaluated their potentiality. Now let's take an honest look at the concept of evangelism as expressed by the church of the 1st century.

THE ORIGINAL COMMAND

Jesus said:

"And ye shall receive power,

AFTER the Holy Spirit has come upon you,

AND you shall be witnesses of me,

BOTH in Jerusalem, and Judea, AND in Samaria,

AND unto the uttermost parts of the earth."

If Jesus were to give this command again today, right here in our country, and you were present to hear . . . what would He say?

First, ask yourself:

What is your Jerusalem?

What was Jerusalem to them in that day?

What is Judea for you?

What was Judea for them?

And what is Samaria?

(Be careful on this one.)

And the uttermost part of the earth?

Jerusalem is the town where you are right now.

Judea—your state, or nation (America).

What about Samaria? I am grateful Jesus didn't forget to include Samaria. We would have! Samaria was *in* Judea. It was segregated. The Samaritans were the outcasts. Today, for us, Samaria is the Indian, the migrant, the negro, the immigrant, the poor, the slum resident, the unlovely.

And "the uttermost parts of the earth?" This has not changed! The whole wide world—for us, as it was for them.

Were those New Testament disciples obedient to the order? What was *their* reaction to this supreme command? What became their plan of action?

Jesus gave the command. He ascended. They returned to Jerusalem (after a little prodding from some angels). They were all filled with the Holy Spirit. Then they set out to obey Jesus. They started with Jerusalem.

The most important question the 20th century church has to ask of the 1st century church is:

HOW DID THEY DO IT?

What did they do to reach *all* of the city of Jerusalem?

It might be better to ask this first: How did they *not* do it?

In the Book of Acts, there are recorded only two mass meetings that could be termed *mass* evangelism. This method really played a minor role in the New Testament church evangelism.

There is another thing they obviously did not do. They did not build buildings and go door to door asking people to "come to church". We need to be reminded that there were *no* church buildings in the New Testament. It isn't even a Biblical concept. Church buildings were not employed until the 3rd century. Today the "church building" concept of evangelism is the greatest single hindrance to world evangelization. *Not* because we have church buildings—but because we won't get *out* of them!

The church building is not the church. The term "church" is not even a New Testament Greek term. The New Testament Greek word was *ecclesia*. We dropped this term in about the 3rd century. We picked up the more formal *Latin* word, *kurcha*. Wherever you see the word, *church*, you read a derivative of Latin, not a derivative of the New Testament Greek.

We must get this straightened out in our minds or suffer eternal consequences. A church building serves one purpose: to keep you from getting cold in winter and hot in summer, or wet when it rains!

This is not an appeal for you to go burn down your church building. Undoubtedly the "church building concept" is necessary for our day. *But get it in its right perspective!* Realize that evangelism is *not* to be centered in the church building. It is to be centered *outside* the church building. The church is not a place to bring the lost *into*, to convert them. It is a battle station—to send Christians *out* from!

JERUSALEM EVANGELIZED

Acts records exactly how they did evangelize Jerusalem. It became the pattern for the church throughout the remainder of the century.

We have read these verses many times. Perhaps they are due a fresh look.

"And they, continuing daily with one accord in the temple, and breaking bread from house to house, did eat their meat with gladness and singleness of heart, praising God, and having favour with all the people. And the Lord added to the church daily such as should be saved."

(Acts 2:46, 47)

Every day the Lord added to the church. The New Testament minimum number of converts a church should win to Christ is 365 per year! At least one a day! There are less than a dozen churches today, out of the quarter of a million churches in America, that get *up to* this New Testament *minimum*.

How did the New Testament church accomplish this feat? They did it in the temple, and in the houses. The 20th century churches have experienced only the first half —in the temple (church).

How could a church average at least one convert a day? There is only one way for men to be saved every day of the year through the ministry of a church. That is for the individual members to win souls *every* day. Any other kind of evangelism, attempting to win souls every day of the year, would completely exhaust itself in a few months. Personal evangelism alone can accomplish this feat.

In Acts 5:42, we see how far they pursued the concept of "house to house evangelism".

"And daily in the temple, and in *every* house,
they ceased not to teach and preach Jesus Christ."

They evangelized *all* of Jerusalem, by going to *all* the homes! In this way, they knew when they had been obedient! This is how to obey Acts 1:8.

Here is a New Testament concept that is so radical, so new, so revolutionary, that it is unbelievable. This is primitive, Biblical evangelism. It has rarely, if ever, crossed the mind of 20th century Christianity:

THE PURPOSE OF THE CHURCH— YOUR CHURCH—IS TO TAKE THE GOSPEL TO EVERY HOUSE IN YOUR TOWN!

Can you say that you have obeyed the Great Commission in your community? Have you evangelized *your* Jerusalem? Have you and your people knocked on every door of every house, every flat, every duplex, every apartment, every garage apartment—every home?! Has your church done this? Be honest, have you ever even thought about doing it?

You can! And you can do it the same way they did! This is the purpose of *your church!* This is the reason for the very existence of your church—to evangelize the entire community. We are not to do it the way we are doing it today, reaching only those who will come to us. You can, you should, and you *must*, launch a drive to totally evangelize your community.

THE PATTERN CONTINUED

In acts 20:20, we see the main thrust of New Testament evangelism continued. (Someone has called Acts 20:20 the 20-20 vision of the church.)

"And how I kept back nothing that was profitable

unto you, but have shewed you, and have taught you publicly, and *from house to house*, testifying both to the Jews, and also to the Greeks, repentance toward God, and faith toward our Lord Jesus Christ."

Here was Paul's pattern. It should be adopted as our pattern to evangelize the world. Paul came into a city and started a church. He stayed for a while to train the Christians in the full Christian life. These Christians, along with Paul, would begin doing what is described in Acts 20:20. Paul would go on to another city as soon as he felt his new Christians were mature. They, in turn, moved in the nearby areas to start churches that would begin doing what they did under Paul.

Here Paul is reminding the leaders of the Ephesian church of his *modus operandi*. He tells them to continue to follow this same plan. The plan: Spend your time going house to house!

From Acts 2 until Acts 20, is a space of about 30 years. Door to door evangelism was the unbroken operation of the church. What were the results?

THE OBEDIENCE TO THE GREAT COMMISSION

Hidden in the 19th chapter of Acts, is one of the most fantastic verses of Scripture in all Holy Writ. For in Acts 19:10, we see obedience to the command of Jesus being carried out in Jerusalem, Judea, Samaria; and more and more of the known world was being reached daily.

"And this continued by the space of *two* years; so that all they which dwelt in Asia heard the word of the Lord Jesus, both Jews and Greeks."

Just think—in two years! That is, 24 months! We have spent the last 200 years trying to win people by other methods. We have hardly held our own, as a result. The last 1800 years of evangelism together can not produce a scene so dramatic as this. In two years—without cars, planes, radio, TV, or printing—*all* of Asia Minor heard the Gospel!

41

That means every person in the teeming city of Damascus. Every person in and around the plains of Jericho. It means Ceasarea, and Nazareth. It means the little villages nestled high in the steep mountains of Lebanon. It means the isolated homes, and even the nomadic tribes of the deserts. In just 24 months!

Talk about revival! This could never have been done by Christians holding mass meetings. In many places, mass meetings would have been outlawed. They did not do it by church buildings. In many cities of that century, had Christians tried to build church buildings, their enemies would have ripped them down.

No, the Christians spilled out of the cities, into the towns, the villages and deserts, until ALL who lived in Asia (Minor) heard the Gospel.

This was the greatest "revival" the world has ever known. And remember, it came through the avenue of *personal* evangelism.

This is the concept that has been lost to us for 1800 years. This is the way they did it then. Let's do it the same way.

THIS IS THE REVIVAL WE REALLY NEED!

CHAPTER 6

WHY PERSONAL EVANGELISM HAS FAILED

Before we say how far personal evangelism can reach and what its impact can be, we must ask another question: Why has personal evangelism failed?

It has. Often a pastor will say: "I have only five or six soul winners in my entire church." He means he has only five or six who have *ever* won a soul to Christ in their entire lives. That is *not* a soul winner.

A young minister said to one of the great pastors of our day, "I have only two soul winners in my church." The elderly minister, pastor of a church with over 3,000 in services every Sunday, replied, "Be thankful, if that is true, for that's two more than I have."

A man who has served as pastor in both the Northern and the Southern United States was asked to compare the difference of the two regions. "In the South," he said, "they talk about soul winning and don't do it. In the North, they don't even talk about it!"

First hand observation convinces me that even the majority of America's Protestant pastors have personally won less than a half a dozen adults to Christ in their entire ministries. This is not even remotely meant to be a criticism. These men want to win souls, desperately. Being human, they are reluctant to talk publicly about failure in such a sensitive and vital area. Let this author hasten to confess that he was a pastor for four years before he ever won one person to Christ personally.

Our definition of "witnessing" has been far too anemic. Often, Christians think that if they invite someone to church, or talk to them about "God", or mention Jesus, or some spiritual topic, then they have "witnessed". There is really no such thing as a witness until you have brought a man to the point where he must decide to accept or reject Jesus Christ as Saviour and Lord.

It has been estimated by Moody Bible Institute that 95 per cent of the Christians in our land have never led a soul to Christ. I am convinced that far less than one per cent of evangelical Christians are *consistent* soul winners.

It is time we admitted that personal evangelism, as it existed in the New Testament, is almost literally nonexistent, anywhere, today. It is also time we set about doing something about it. Something new, revolutionary and different is needed, *now!* For what we have done in the past has *not* cured the ailment!

There has not been a time in modern history when there was a sweeping movement of personal soul winning. The present day Christian has never seen it; our fathers have never seen it; nor their fathers before them.

There was never an hour when it was more needed!

There is really no way to know or guess what a return to soul winning on the part of a large portion of Christians across this country could accomplish. We have absolutely no rule of thumb to go by. We can only guess. We have never seen the church "revived" through a return to soul winning. We have no way to know how deep such a revival could be, how great its impact, or how long it would last. A search through 1,000 years of history will produce scarcely a hint of what happens when a great number of Christians begin going everywhere winning souls to Jesus Christ.

We do not know—But let us pray that this generation will be privileged to find out!

BUT WHY THIS FAILURE?

Why, though, has personal evangelism so completely failed to be revived? Why is it not today the main thrust and consuming occupation of the church? To understand this problem is the first step to experiencing the solution.

I. The Wrong Concept In Soul Winning

The first reason for the failure of personal evangelism is perhaps the major factor for all the ensuing reasons.

The method is wrong. It won't work!

It's that simple.

It is to be kept in mind that God uses men, not

methods; but the right man with the wrong methods is as ineffective as the wrong man with the right method. Try as you will, square wheels will not roll.

Incredible as it seems, it was less than 70 years ago that the first book on soul winning was ever written. Just 70 years. This in itself is proof that we are only on the threshold of rediscovering personal evangelism.

The book was written by R. A. Torrey. Torrey was one of the greatest Christians of the 19th (or any) century. His books are all classics. His life was anointed with the power of God. His teachings, on a dozen subjects, were immeasurable contributions to theology.

But as a soul winner, Torrey was an individualist. He was a man without complexes. He knew no fear. We have all known a few men like him. They can use any method, under any situation, with anybody, and win them to Christ. Torrey could walk up to anybody and say, "Are you saved?" They would not be offended. He would probably win them to Jesus.

For every one Christian who can witness like that, there are one million who cannot. (Oh, we can try. Most of us do . . . once . . . but our failure is so great and so bitter, it usually ends our career as a soul winner at the very outset.)

If you have ever read Torrey's book, *How To Bring Men To Christ*, you may note that the entire scheme of it was developed, and used almost exclusively, in the INQUIRY ROOM of the Moody campaigns.

Torrey wrote the book for the inquiry rooms.

This, in itself, makes it inept for general witnessing. An inquiry room where men have deliberately come to be converted, is anything but the situation you face in everyday witnessing, at a factory, or in a home.

Nonetheless, this method alone has prevailed. It

has been taught in virtually every Bible institute and seminary in the world.

The author owns almost every book written in the English language on soul winning. There are hundreds. Virtually every one of them is a re-write of Torrey's book. Incredibly, I know several great soul winners who have been commissioned by their denominations to write a book on soul winning. Now these men never employ the Torrey method, but they have written along the Torrey line, inadvertently, so deeply ingrained is the tradition!

We have depended on this one method exclusively. Even people who know nothing of the origin of this method follow it completely, for it is all we have ever known. Almost all of us fall into this method as young Christians, without ever knowing it is a "method". Most people have never even stopped to consider that there could be another way.

Most of us are ordinary people, with no outstanding ability. Let us admit it: most Christians are timid. An attempt at direct personal soul winning is a horrifying experience for all of us. And the Torrey method just plain *will not work* for ordinary, timid Christians.

>   (All readers who are not ordinary, timid,
>   and who experience absolutely no fear of
>   witnessing, need read no further!)

Most of us just cannot remember and quote Scriptures under pressure. We do not excel in reasoning nor in argumentative and persuasive ability. We have not the knack for beginning a spiritual conversation bluntly, nor do we have the keen perception to ask unanswerable questions, and lead a man down a long series of logical, unanswerable conclusions. We are not logicians.

That is the Torrey method. But for most of us: we're scared; we stutter; we can't reason well; we can't remember facts, answers, faces, or names. We lose arguments. And we almost faint at the thought of even trying. To say the least, we don't perform too well under pressure.

No wonder we can't win souls!

Attempt to apply this 19th century method in the home of a lost man here in the latter part of the 20th century, and you find that it goes completely contrary to the grain of both the lost person and the would-be soul winner. We live in a different sociological era for witnessing.

I would like to add that I do not know a great, consistently effective soul winner in America today who actually employs this method when he himself witnesses.

11. The Poor Example Of Some Soul Winners

Everyone has a stereotype idea of what certain groups of people are like. Perhaps the stereotype of the soul winner, to many, is this: a man with a wild look, wrinkled shirt, and mussed hair, walking up to some innocent bystander, grabbing him by the collar, lifting him off his feet, staring at him with beady eyes and, in a doom's day voice, saying: "Say, brother, do you know God?"

The repulsive manner and method of many good intention Christians who have a love and zeal (without knowledge) has made many more sensitive Christians disclaim any part of it. Some have even, because of this, spoken against personal soul winning and tried to find some Scriptural basis for exemption.

This need not be!

A parallel can be drawn with the salesman. Fifty years ago, many salesmen were the brash, fast talking, foot-in-the-door type. About 30 years ago, sales methods began to be refined. Today we are told that these refined methods have affected the public relations of many areas of society. What happened to sales methods should—and must—happen to soul winning methods. They need a revision.

It is possible for the most refined and sensitive Christians to witness and win souls to Christ in a natural, relaxed manner, with a perfect stranger. It can be done every day. Obviously, though, not by the concepts we have employed in the past.

The soul winner deserves, and is due, a better public image.

III. The Wrong Kind Of Training

There is another really big reason why we have not experienced a mighty sweep of effective witnessing. Our training and teaching methods have been woefully inadequate.

Have you ever heard it said, "The only way to learn to be a soul winner is to get a Bible and go out and start witnessing?" We all have. Have you ever heard it said, "The only way to become a physician is to get a pocket knife and start cutting people open?" No? Well, one statement contains as much wisdom as the other.

A soldier learns to fight by receiving every kind of training: instruction, observation, practice, simulated conditions, etc. So does an astronaut, a doctor, a pilot, etc. Why not a soul winner?

Our schools and churches have tried to teach everything by the *lecture method*. This is great for theology, and any of the abstract sciences. Soul winning is in the field of the practical sciences, not the abstract. The lecture method alone can never prepare a man for the gruelling experience of soul winning.

There is a vast training gap that exists today between a lecture delivered on "How to Win Souls", and the moment Christians are sent out to witness. This gap must be closed. It must be bridged by a whole new concept in soul winning training.

Even such a bed-rock practical thing as "How to Visit in a Home" has found its way into only a few books in the last decade, and even then in sketchy, outline form. Such skimpy treatment cannot possibly make a timid Christian into a confident, proficient visitor.

Lectures delivered on soul winning, embracing our archive methods of witnessing, were bound to produce small results.

IV. Personal Evangelism Has Occupied The Wrong Position In Evangelism

Soul winning has occupied a secondary position in evangelism. Even its most zealous exponents often relegate it to that secondary position, unwittingly.

For instance, soul winning is always emphasized strongly right before an evangelistic campaign. Look what this does to perennial witnessing, psychologically. It relegates it to a position far below mass evangelism—as a primer, or aid. Too, it makes soul winning a *seasonal* affair. It puts it on a "rush" or "sandwiched" basis, to be squeezed in right before the campaign. This position keeps personal evangelism from ever becoming a basis for "revival" in itself. By the process of elimination, mass evangelism has become, ever since the days of Wesley, the sole conduit of "revival" among Christians.

Look at it this way: when we have an evangelistic campaign, months are spent in prayer; hundreds of dollars are spent on publicity; for weeks the church is a beehive of activity; and expectation mounts to the skies.

A church which plans an "enlargement campaign" in an effort to produce a strong perennial program of enlistment evangelism, goes to elaborate ends training teachers and workers in every area of this science. Frequently the modern day church hires a full time staff worker who has received thousands of hours of seminary training in the vast scope of enlistment evangelism.

But when we go to train soul winners? What do we do?

We teach a book!

Almost every day we read of great, mammoth plans for evangelistic campaigns in mass evangelism that entail unbelievable amounts of time, money and preparation. Have you ever heard of such extensive plans for a campaign in Personal Evangelism? Better still, have you ever even heard of a Campaign in Personal Evangelism!

Here is another fact that highlights the neglect of personal evangelism: today there are literally thousands of young men giving their lives, full time, as evangelists in the ministry of mass evangelism. There are many, many young men going into a ministry that is primarily a ministry of enlistment evangelism. There is a growing number of Christian "Education Directors" every year. For some denominations, they rival in number the men going into the pastorates.

Both of these areas of evangelism have received the highest attention. They have been studied and prepared for as exacting sciences. No such attention has ever been shown Personal Evangelism.

At this writing, as far as I know, there are only three men in North America who are giving themselves to a ministry of conducting Campaigns in Personal Evangelism (teaching and training laymen and sending them out in vast house-to-house soul winning efforts). And this is only *one* area of the potential of full time service in personal evangelism. There are many different ways a young man could give his entire life in personal evangelism. These fields are open, men are needed and wanted, urgently.

If there were one-tenth of the number of talented, dedicated, Spirit-filled young men in the field of personal evangelism, that there are in mass evangelism, we could see a revival and a turning to God sweep this continent, unlike anything in modern times.

Our neglect of Personal Evangelism has been woeful.

V. A Lack Of Emphasis On The Spirit-Filled Life

Unlike mass evangelism, which calls for only the evangelist to be Spirit-filled, personal evangelism is so demanding on the individual Christian, that it is a real test of spiritual tinsel. This may be the greatest single reason for a lack of return to Personal Evangelism.

It is hard to say which has caused what: a lack of emphasis on soul winning causing a lack in emphasis on the Spirit-filled life; or the reverse. Nonetheless, there must be a re-emphasis of both. A vital experience with the Holy Spirit is absolutely necessary for a return to soul winning.

There cannot be, there never will be, a turning to personal witnessing among men who are not Spirit filled.

Being a Spirit-filled Christian remains in the realm of the mysterious for most Christians. Yet it was God's way of giving victory in the problem of daily living. It need not be so mysterious. Every Christian could know the joy of constantly walking in the Spirit.

VI. An Unnatural Attitude Toward Soul Winning

All the preceding problems have combined to produce another one. There is a wide-spread feeling that winning people to Christ is very difficult and almost impossible; that the unsaved are Gospel hardened, and uninterested in knowing Jesus Christ; and only a few will respond to Him.

There is also a mysterious flavor about it—a belief that only the "giant Christian" (Wesley, Moody, Spurgeon, etc.) can win souls; that it is outside the realm of ordinary earthlings.

This is all incorrect. Soul winning is simple, and the most timid little lady in your church can be as effective as anyone in winning multitudes to Jesus.

There are also misconceptions such as: "You've got to have a burden for souls". There are no Scriptural grounds for this—no New Testament hint of such an idea. You don't train a soldier to fight, order him into battle, then hear him say, "I'm waiting for a burden". We're under orders to go, burden or no!

VII. Lack Of Spiritual Preparation

As pointed out, we make great spiritual preparation for other kinds of evangelism. God's spiritual laws are unalterable. We must learn that spiritual preparation is absolutely necessary here, too.

A breakthrough in the problems just outlined could well unleash the dormant power of soul winning, and send it blazing across the globe!

CHAPTER 7

WHAT CAN PERSONAL EVANGELISM DO?

We are all familiar with what happens to a church when God uses mass evangelism as His instrument for revival. What could we expect results to be if we see a return of personal evangelism in our generation?

1. Personal Evangelism Can Bring About Revival.

Every book that the author has ever read on "revival", speaks about revival in the church coming through the preaching of the Word in mass evangelism.

But mass evangelism is not necessarily the only avenue of revival! Personal evangelism can be the instrument through which revival comes, just as much. Indeed, more, for revival through the instrument of personal evangelism is deeper.

Why?

Because it is the one revival which removes the Christian from the position of a spectator.

Most outpourings of the Spirit have been experienced when a crowd of people felt a collective season' of repentance, perhaps confession, and joy. But this is temporal. It lacks roots of maturity. Nothing has happened that has actually given them growth in Christ. There is lacking a strong foundation upon which it can be sustained. Most revival spirit wanes soon after the evangelist has moved on. The people sat, experiencing a cleansing and revival spirit, but nothing happened which could sustain their experience.

When revival comes through personal evangelism, it is the *individual* who experiences the impact, rather than an evangelist. The layman himself is the instrument of the Holy Spirit. When revival comes, it is not dependent on a certain location (the church building), or a personality (the evangelist), or other people (the gathering). The spirit of revival is sustained in the Christian's heart as long as he goes on bearing fruit.

An experience in soul winning has the unique quality of producing a desire in the Christian to do more of the same! The layman is lifted up out of the position, where he has been for hundreds of years, of being a "hearer of the Word only". Suddenly, he is a "doer of the Word".

The author has personally seen a great spirit of revival come to a church, when only a handful were won to Christ through soul winning. The impact on the lives of the soul winners was so great that an entire church experienced revival. It is the personal quality of witnessing that makes this difference. An individual can become very excited when he's the one it happened to!

There is an innocent excitement and expectancy that seems to say: "This didn't happen to someone else—it happened to *me!*"

No vicarious thrill here; this is personal.

2. The Spirit Of Revival Can Be Sustained.

This is the one unique element of personal evangelism. The revival and the evangelism produced can both be conserved.

Once the heart of a pastor or layman is set on fire by winning souls, that spirit can be continued. The joy need not be seasonal. Winning of souls keeps a Christian closer to Christ in his own daily living. Witnessing is the very expression of the normal, abundant life. A tree bears fruit *only* out of the richness and overflow of its life. *It has more than it can contain*, so it must produce fruit.

Walk into any "dead" church. Sit on the platform. Look out over the congregation. The congregation sits there in an almost hypnotic state. Everyone is expressionless. Why?

There is no expectancy.

No one really expects to meet God, or see His power! Week after week, nothing really ever happens in the church. This "spell" may be temporarily broken once a year, when an evangelist comes.

On the other hand, a church that is winning souls is on pins and needles constantly, waiting expectantly to see what God will do next. Pastors who have seen their own lives and their church revived through the instrument of personal evangelism, have often reported·

> "I now preach with an unction I've never
> before experienced. The people wait, ex-
> pectantly, to see God move."

There is nothing more exciting for a Christian than to come to church and look across the aisle at a new convert he has won to Christ, sitting there with the radiance of redemption on his face. A church like this cannot be dead!

Another characteristic of a church that starts winning souls is that it miraculously loses a guilt complex. Unknowingly, most pastors and churches have a guilt complex for not winning souls. Losing this complex is one of the greatest possible experiences of freedom. Failure to recognize the existence of this quilt complex is destroying us.

This generation has prayed for revival more than any other. Perhaps God has withheld revival from us until now, simply because He does not want us to go through some emotional experience that will pass and soon leave us bored because we cannot live on a high level of spiritual frenzy. God wants to send a *sustained revival* that can last and spread, and reach a whole world.

This is truly the revival we need.

3. Personal Evangelism Can Evangelize The World.

The word "evangelize" does not denote winning the world to Christ, but presenting the Gospel until every man has had an opportunity to decide for or against Christ.

Until now, we have tried to get the mountain to come to us. It is so much easier to go to the mountain. We have tried to evangelize the world by using the massive media for quick results, but each year we are farther from our goal.

We dare not ever hope to win the world to Christ until we have regained a strong emphasis on personal witnessing. We cannot expect the men who go as missionaries to evangelize the world without this instrument. They must first have an experience with personal evangelism in their own lives back home. Missionaries work under a severe handicap because they do not come from soul winning churches, and have never experienced revival through personal Christianity in action. Therefore, they have no way to carry such experience to the mission field. Our missionaries can be no greater than the churches they come from.

Personal evangelism is that one principle of evangelism which can be employed throughout the world to reach every man on this planet.

4. Soul Winning Begets Soul Winners.

Men who are won to Christ by a personal witness are always the most responsive to becoming soul winners themselves. This is a fact that is not often observed. The ground for multiplication is very fertile.

5. Personal Evangelism Grows Christians.

An outstanding evangelist who has given most of his life to mass evangelism, but who recently began giving his full time to a unique ministry in personal evangelism, confided this to the author:

"In all the years of my evangelistic ministry, I never received over three or four letters per year from Christians thanking me for the influence of my ministry on their lives. Since going full time into personal evangelism, it is not unusual to get 15 such letters per week!"

If you are to win a soul to Christ you must put into play the whole Christian life: the Word; prayer; dependence on the Holy Spirit, all the fruits of maturity in Christ. It is a constant challenge. New experience keeps the Christian's testimony fresh and alive. How can any of us be happy in Christ when nothing *really* new has happened since our conversion! A consistent witness walks in the manifest power of God . . . daily.

We have many people who are great *church members*, but who are exceedingly weak *Christians*. When these church members begin to win souls, you will notice they shift their area of devotion. A greater love for the Person of Jesus Christ springs up.

Christians are really changed when they win souls.

6. Personal Evangelism Is The Most Productive Evangelism Of All.

This is a revealing fact to many, but we have consistently seen more people find Christ—and come into the church—through crusades in Personal Evangelism, than are being won to Christ through any similar campaigns in mass evangelism.

Percentage wise, based on the number of Christians actually participating, personal evangelism is always far and away the most fruitful means of evangelism.

Perhaps the day will come when personal evangelism can stand on an equal footing with mass evangelism in the number of people and churches participating. Should the day ever come, when great hosts of churches unite to evangelize entire cities through house to house witnessing, THE CHURCH WILL SEE THE LARGEST INGATHERING OF SOULS IN ALL CHRISTIAN HISTORY.

If someone were to ask you to describe "revival", what would you say? Perhaps something like this:

> "Christians would be going everywhere, talking about Jesus to everyone. Every human being in the city would be conscious of, and be encountering, the message of Christ. Multitudes would be finding Christ. There would be a spirit of expectancy everywhere. Christians would be testifying—to the banker, the carpenter, the barber, everyone. A whole city would be convicted. Joy and power would sweep over the churches, and Christ would be magnified."

Well, sir, that is a description of personal evangelism in action!!

CHAPTER 8

GREAT SOUL WINNING CHURCHES OF OUR DAY

Let's take a look at a few of the greatest soul winning churches of our day. There are a few churches that stand out as leaders in personal evangelism. These churches are the Einsteins and the Rembrandts of their field. They bear close study. I would like to suggest that the Evangelism Department of every denomination in America make a very close and intense study of these churches. All the theory on earth can't match actual success. These churches have made some great discoveries that we all ought to understand and adapt to our own use.

On Wednesday night, the author walked into one such church, located in Texas. The church was celebrating its fifth anniversary. The pastor had been there four of those five years.

Four years previously, 44 people had been present to extend a call to this young man to become their pastor. They were meeting in a garage at that time. In the four years that followed, the church grew from an attendance of 44, to an attendance that reached as high as 2,000. Their annual budget had gone from $6,000 a year to nearly $200,000 per year. Their property had been worth $6,000 in the beginning. Four years later, the property was worth one million dollars. In its five year history, the church had outgrown five buildings.

One question was waiting to be answered: Why was this church one of the fastest growing churches in the world? I asked the pastor this question, as we walked together to the auditorium that Wednesday evening.

In the first year of its history, the church had won ten people to Christ. When this young man became their new pastor, he announced that whatever else was done, this church would do one thing: it would win souls. He trained about ten of his men and started going out door to door with them. From this, he developed a visitation program. The first year he was there the church brought 150 converts into its fellowship through (water) baptism. The next year, there were some 300 new Christians added to the church.* The next year, around 500, and the next year, 702. (A year later there were 643 new converts added to the church by baptism.) The pastor jokingly remarked, "I've got more ushers passing out offering plates now than I had members when I started here!" Counting missionaries and their children, this church was sponsoring 44 people on the mission field . . . exactly the number they had in attendance four years earlier.

After I had asked him my question, he said: "Come into the church and I will *show* you the reason for our church's growth." There in the Wednesday evening service, by actual head count, were over 700 people. The pastor went to the platform and asked, "How many of you have won someone to Jesus through our visitation program in the last twelve months?" Three hundred people stood up.

You do not have to be a mathematician to figure out why this church was one of the fastest growing churches of this century.

———

At another time, it was my privilege to sit down with the man who has the distinction and honor of baptizing, in water, more new converts every year than any other man in the world. His church probably wins more people to Christ than any other church on earth.

When I asked this question: "Why is it that your church brings more new Christians into its fellowship than any other church in the world?" he replied, "If there is any earthly answer, it is simply this: "my people win souls."

* In 1959 the author did research on the leading evangelistic churches in the world. Here was what he was able to discover: About 200 churches won as many as 100 people to Christ. (There are over a quarter of a million churches in America alone). Only 13 churches won over 200 people. Only 6 won over 300 people to Christ.

In four words, he had given the key.

I once read a letter from this man, which he had written to a pastor in the West. In it he made this statement: "I have emphasized one truth in my church over and over. I have repeated it until my people have finally come to believe it." He went on to say that his main emphasis was:

"And daily in the temple and *every* house,
they ceased not to teach and to preach Jesus
Christ."

Here is a church that actually visits in the home of every family that moves into the city! The church is located in a city of well over a million people. The church has five visitation programs per week. It has visited and contacted as many as 10,000 people in one week.

How?

The pastor has told us. He has taken one truth and emphasized it until the people have come to believe it. They actually believe they should win souls; therefore, they do. The pastor has exemplified it in his own life. He preaches it every time he stands in the pulpit. He has never stopped emphasizing it. There came a moment, finally, when it clicked in the minds of his people, and this became their one, magnificent obsession. Last year that church won to Christ, and actually brought into its fellowship, over 1,400 new converts. (This means that almost every Sunday, somewhere between ten and fifteen new Christians came forward to publicly confess Christ.)

———

Then there is another church with a remarkable ministry. On the Sunday of this particular visit, I was accompanied by my very lovely wife. We sat in an auditorium that seated perhaps four to five thousand people. The pastor stood to preach. Being honest, we can guess that his message that morning was probably below par. But as we stood at the close of the service, the pastor gave an open invitation—a very simple one. In five minutes, we saw a scene that transformed that service into as wonderful a revival as most of us have ever been privileged to behold. Right in front of where we sat, a man stood up and started down the aisle. A Christian stepped out and took him by the arm and accompanied him down the aisle. Someone seated beside my wife stood and made his way out of the pew, down the aisle. Once more, a Christian stepped out with him. Then someone else behind us; then from all over the auditorium. I began to count—ten, twenty, thirty, forty! In less than five minutes—without any pleading—without even a word being said to encourage decisions—forty people walked down the aisles of that church to unite with it in one way or another. (We were later told that in the evening service some 20 others went forward.) I stood there with tears running down my face as I watched this unbelievable, scene that morning.

At the end of the service, I rushed up to the platform and grabbed one of the staff members by the arm and asked: "Can you tell me how many people you had out for visitation last week?"

He shrugged his shoulders nonchalantly and said, "No, I don't know, I forgot to count them."

Then I asked, "Well, *about* how many?"

His answer was, "Oh, I don't really know. About 500 I guess."

"Thanks", I answered, "that's all I needed to know!"

You can't get around it. This is the *one* New Testament answer.

Then there's a church in New Orleans. Very few people know the pastor, that is, on a nationwide scale. He is a very quiet, and if you met him you would probably say, a very ordinary person. He is very modest. We might wish, though, that his ministry and methods were known better and understood by every pastor.

His church has won more people to Christ, on a yearly average, than any other church in the Southern Baptist Convention.

The author heard one of the leaders in the Department of Evangelism of the Southern Baptist Convention ask him this question: "You do most of your soul winning by enlisting people in the Sunday School, don't you?"

His answer was, "No, we win almost no one to Christ by enlisting them into the Sunday School. You see, we live in a very strong Roman Catholic community. We can get almost no one to come to our church. This is one of the reasons our church is a soul winning church! We were forced into the position of winning them to Christ in their homes. Then after Jesus transforms them, they come."

Every year this church brings into its fellowship somewhere between three and four hundred new converts. This does not include literally hundreds that are won to Christ who join other churches, and those that they are not able to bring into any Protestant church.

How does he do it? He is the first to admit that it is not by great oratory. He has a group of faithful Christians in his church, somewhere between fifty and one hundred fifty every week, going out to knock on doors. They sit down with the lost and win them to Jesus Christ, in their homes.

———

Now, these have all been large churches, and perhaps someone is saying, "I'm pastor of a small church."

Yes, but remember, these churches were once small, too. Furthermore, the same thing can happen in the smallest rural areas in the world. I watched it happen in my own church.

Lets look at another church and another man, just about twenty-four years old, who pastored in a rural community in East Texas. The little church sits out in an "open rural community". (This simply means there's no town.) The pastor once jokingly said, "You can stand on the roof of the church and see two houses, and that's all there are!" When the church called him, the attendance there was about 75. The entire area probably had no more than 400 people in it. The new pastor took a religious census immediately, and in the entire community, found exactly six people who were lost. "These six," he said, "were what you would call Gospel hardened."

You could never guess what happened.

In the next two years, that church went from an attendance of 75 to over 350 people in Sunday School. In those 2 years the church won over 300 people to Christ.

Now what happened? That young "preacher boy" simply decided that the field was the whole world, and not just the community around him. He went all over that end of the entire county, knocking on doors and winning people to Christ. Soon his people were following suit. They would drive to towns nearby—fifteen and twenty-five miles away—to win souls to Jesus Christ. At the end of two years, that church had three buses that were picking up some 200 people and bringing them to Sunday School!

There is no limitation in the winning of souls, if a man's vision is big enough. The field *is* the world.

———

Each one of these churches is a great romantic story in itself. Whole communities have been transformed by the ministry of the Christians who are the products of these churches. Story after story could be told of the miraculous transformation that has come to the wealthiest and to the most ignominious, because someone cared enough to come to them and win them to Christ. Week after week, these new Christians stand to testify of what Jesus Christ did for them through the ministry of laymen who have discovered the secret of soul winning. Week after week, you see the consistent thrill and joy of Christians who are constantly bearing fruit as "doers of the Word of God".

You walk away realizing that this is the kind of life that Jesus Christ designed for each one of us. Not a rollercoaster spiritual life, but a consistent life of bearing fruit. A life of joy—constant, new, refreshing testimonies. And you also walk away with the amazing conviction that everything you read in the Book of Acts is just as possible today as it ever was.

Each of these great churches stands as proof that what happened in the church in Jerusalem 2,000 years ago, can happen in our day too! May we have more such churches.

WHAT DO SOUL WINNING CHURCHES HAVE IN COMMON?

Soon after completing seminary training, it was this author's privilege to make a study of the outstanding soul winning churches in America. The question if often asked, "What makes those churches different?" or "What do these churches have in common?"

Many other questions have been asked about these churches. Most of them are the same questions I asked the pastors of these churches. Questions like this:

"How do I get started?" "How do you train the people?" "*What* do you train them?" "How do you get them out to visitation?" "How do you keep them coming out to visitation?"

These are perhaps some of the questions you were asking when you picked up this book. These are logical questions to ask.

For instance: Each of these pastors has a deep sense of purpose, and a genuine love for souls (and this is one of those things that just can't be artificial). Each of these men has a personal desire to win souls. They express a determination that if nothing else on earth ever happens, they and their people will win souls. These men live and breathe, eat and sleep, with just one thought. As they stand in the pulpit, the messages they bring, as they make their announcements, as they plan their church program, as they talk to their people, there is one underlying, unshakable, unmovable thought: "We must win souls."

Without this obsession, there is no soul winning pastor, and without this, there is no soul winning church.

Once, while driving through the country with one of

these great soul winning pastors, I counted five people he talked to about Christ in just 30 miles.

What gives a man such a natural desire to win others? This is one spiritual quality a man just can't "play act". In each case, I found the same answer. Each of these men has had a profound experience with God. For the reader of this book, and for every minister, this is the first qualification you must have in your own life.

Here are some four areas that each church has in common with the others. (For the most part, these pastors do not know one another):

1. A Simplified Church Program.

This quality sticks out so obviously. Pick up the bulletin, or listen to the announcements. These churches have an absolute minimum of activities. This is one of the great secrets to having a soul winning church. A church that has many activities, never gives the people a chance to come to grips with one or two great truths. Churches with a multitude of activities only reflect the lack of singleminded purpose in the life of the pastor. A church that has a program jammed with activities is actually creating competition with its program in soul winning. A church that puts on a study course one week; a week-end evangelistic campaign the next; a stewardship emphasis the next three weeks; a Sunday School enlargement campaign the next two weeks; a drive to reach a foreign mission offering goal the next week; an evangelistic campaign the next week; a high attendance day the next week—cannot possibly hope to have a consistent program of soul winning.

We can put forth this proposition: you must choose between doing many things poorly, or a few things well. Is it not possible, that if we would do a few things well—like winning men to Christ—most other activities of the church would actually lose their meaning and become unnecessary?

A profound statement was once made by one of
the great old Christian giants of the last generation:

"I have never met a great man, but what
he was possessed with *one* great vision."

2. Visitation Is Church Wide

The second thing that you will notice about these
churches is: their program of visitation is not *enlistment evangelism*. Visitation is for everyone, regardless of what class they are members. It is not just
the teachers that come to visitation. It is not just
the officers of the Sunday School that are out winning souls, but it is everyone's job. As far as I can
recall, I do not know of one of these *consistently*
great soul winning churches that makes visitation assignments according to Sunday School classes. Nor
when they go out is the first thought in their mind
to "invite them to Sunday School". Their first
thought is to win these people to Jesus Christ.
Church membership and enrolling in Sunday School
come after that. Enrollment in Sunday School is
second, not first.

One of these pastors was asked: "Do you get
many unsaved prospects from your Sunday School
enrollment?" The answer was astonishing.

"No," he said.

"We cover the entire city so well that we
know almost everyone and their relationship
to Christ. Our Sunday School yields almost
no conversions. Our people are so versed in
winning souls, that anyone who comes to our
church as often as three times in a row, is
usually won to Christ by some layman."

This is the way it ought to be! If every Sunday
School teacher in your church were a soul winner
there would be little need for enlistment evangelism.

3. The third common factor is that each of these

churches has a CONSTANT PROGRAM OF SOUL WINNING TRAINING.

Nearly all these churches give one or two weeks of each year to soul winning training, and one or two solid weeks of soul winning visiting.

Each pastor has provided a class in soul winning instruction that is kept in continuous operation. New church members can come in and receive extensive training in soul winning methods, and others can take a "refresher" course.

In closing we repeat the main observation made before: each of these pastors exemplifies all that he asks others to do, by being a constant winner of men.

CHAPTER 9

A REVIVAL OF
PERSONAL EVANGELISM IN OUR GENERATION

In the last few years we have been seeing the fore-glimpse of a revival of Personal Evangelism. This chapter seeks to briefly report some of these events.

In 1900, it was the largest church of the city. By 1959, it was deserted and boarded up. For two years, there had not been a service in it. The church had died.

At the turn of the century, an average Sunday in this church had seen 800 people coming to worship. Through the years, this elite church, in one of the nicest residential areas of the city, began to go down. The wealthy people moved away, poor people came in. Soon many Spanish Americans were moving in, too. The denomination itself became alarmed about the condition of this famous church. Several very intensive programs were launched to bring it back to life. But nothing succeeded. The grand old building finally lay empty.

In 1959, a young preacher came to the city who claimed the call of God upon his life. He was just a young man, 24 years old, very gay and optimistic. You could almost call him immature. (But there was one thing in his life that turned out to be a big advantage in his favor: being young, he had never learned how to do things the wrong way!)

He found that there were only seven members left in the church. He got them together and announced, "I want to be your pastor; vote me in." (And sure enough they did!)

He went to a Mexican orphanage nearby and arranged to have the little children come to the church there on Sunday morning to worship. When the pastor contacted me, he was running 50 in Sunday School—forty little orphans, seven members, and his family.

He invited me to hold a campaign in his church. He

asked that his people be trained to win souls. He wanted to inaugurate a program of soul winning visitation in his church.

The scene was unique: a magnificent old building, which would easily seat 1,000 people, and there on the front row, ten Christians learning how to win souls. The meeting closed on Friday, and I flew to another campaign. What happened was unbelievable.

Four Sundays later, that little church had gone from an attendance of 50 to an attendance of 220!

Now what had happened?

The houses were the same. The same people lived there who had been there for years. Revival struck that church in those four weeks, but there had been no evangelist or evangelistic campaign. What had happened? Nothing except this: those ten Christians went out every night for one solid week, visiting in homes, winning people to Jesus Christ. The next week, they went out, and the next week. The pastor jokingly said over the telephone, "I've got a problem no other preacher on earth has. My people don't want to do anything but win souls!"

How would you like to have that for a problem?

Before the year was out, that little church had won more Spanish American people to Jesus Christ than all the rest of the evangelical churches in the city put together, as well as winning a large number of Anglos. Out of the nearly 60 churches of the same denomination in that city, this little church ranked at the top for the number won to Christ.

———

In Los Angeles, a two-week campaign was conducted in Personal Evangelism. The first week, the author trained the Christians in the art of visiting and soul winning. The second week was under the direction of the pastor. This church had won about 40 people to Christ the year before. Enthusiasm in the first week (the week of training) was at an all time high. The pastor and his people set a goal to evangelize "the world of our community". They set as their task, to witness in the home of every person in that community of 40,000 people.

About two weeks after the campaign, the pastor died of a heart attack. The associate pastor was called to become pastor. Even with this very difficult set back, in the next two months, that church brought into its fellowship, 67 new *families*. The church experienced the most incredible revival that city ever witnessed, as those people went out winning people to Christ. God overruled the most difficult circumstances, to sweep the church with a vibrant spirit of revival.

———

In Portland, Oregon, a city-wide Campaign in Personal Evangelism was being planned. It was sponsored by some 50 churches in that city. The author flew up to Portland two months ahead of the campaign for a Preparation Meeting with the pastors and committees. While there, a brief time was spent teaching soul winning in one of the co-operating churches. The two months passed. When I arrived back there for the Campaign, the pastor of the church which had received the brief advance training, told of a remarkable experience.

On Sunday night following their brief training, he walked into the church and announced that he was dismissing the Sunday evening service. Instead of having a regular church service he sent them out to witness! Then they decided to continue for the next three nights. The spirit of soul winning caught fire, and a program of soul winning visiting was commenced. We were all stunned, and then deeply grateful, when the pastor reported this fact: "Already three people have gone to be with Jesus, whom we had won to Christ since you were here two months ago." I have often shuddered to think what happens every day because churches have not had this experience, and how many are going out to meet God unprepared, who otherwise might have been won.

Recently a nation-wide publication ran the story of what God had done in Portland. This pastor recounted the first meeting in his church, and then the city-wide campaign. Following this, he told some of the countless stories of wonderful conversion experiences, because the laymen of the church were winning souls everywhere.

In a brief period of less than three months, the laymen in that church had won over 200 souls to Jesus Christ!

In a town of about 45,000 people, a church set three weeks aside to have an intensive soul winning campaign. The purpose was to evangelize their city. The first week was given over entirely to training in soul winning. The next 2 weeks were given over to visiting. In twelve days of visiting—following a systematic, prearranged plan—the people of that church visited all the hospitals, old folks homes, and all other places of convalescing in the city. The ladies were in charge of this phase of the program, and went from bed to bed witnessing.

The men witnessed, person to person, in the jails, in the rescue missions, making a special emphasis to witness in slum areas. They went to the "flop houses" (places where transients, bums, and derelicts pay something like 15 cents to 25 cents per night for a cot).

Of course, the main thrust of the two weeks of soul winning was in "house to house" evangelism. Every night for twelve nights, Christians went into homes and witnessed of their Saviour. When the two weeks of visiting were over, 333 people had been led to Christ, by actual count. In the next three Sundays, that church received 150 new Christians into its fellowship!

Later, the pastor made this incredible remark to me:

"Our visitation program is large enough now that we can visit every home in this city about every two months."

Even more than that, this campaign set in motion a permanent and sustained program of soul winning in the hearts of scores of laymen. When the campaign was over, people who had never won souls in their lives before would never stop witnessing again as long as they live.

This is revival—the most powerful, productive, New Testament spirit of revival that is possible for a people to experience.

There are many stories, too numerous to recount. For instance, the young student who attended a city-wide campaign in personal evangelism in Seattle, Washington, and returned to his Bible college and organized the "Evangelaires", for the purpose of training laymen and winning souls themselves. In one month, these young students (ten of them) won 50 people to Christ.

Or the 19 churches in a South Texas city that went together for a Crusade In Personal Evangelism. The meeting was held in the midst of a state-wide scandal over drug traffic, gambling and prostitution centered in this city. During the second week of the campaign, and in the weeks to follow, many of the most prominent names involved in this scandal of dope and prostitution—along with some of the most notorious names in that sea coast town—were won to Christ. They stood in the churches and publicly acknowledged both their deeds, and the transforming power of Christ.

Or a church in Missouri that had only two additions by profession of faith during an entire year. The next year, after experiencing a real awakening in personal evangelism, over 100 people were led to Christ in that small community.

And the West Texas church (rather sedate at that) which, on the closing Sunday of a thrust to evangelize its community, was forced to move its Sunday morning service out of the church auditorium into the high school auditorium across the street, because of the size of the crowd. There, 50 people responded publicly to the invitation. Almost all had been won in the homes during the week.

This does not include the thousands of stories of individual laymen who, having tasted of this revival, and, refusing to allow it to die in their own lives, have gone on to win loved ones, and friends, and strangers. They have won them in such places as death row, taverns, houses of ill fame, and even in the halls of our state and federal government, in offices, factories, on streets, among the very wealthy in the residential areas, and in the slums among the very poorest.

Beyond this, many of these laymen and women have gone on to preach and testify of the transformation in their own lives. Some have turned about to teach others what they have learned, fulfilling Paul's admonition to "commit thou to faithful men, who shall be able to teach others also."

Perhaps this is the most significant thing of all: these experiences *have not* died down, but burn brighter every day in the hearts of those who experience them.

PART II

PROBLEMS AND PRINCIPLES
OF A
SOUL WINNING CHURCH

CHAPTER 10

THE SOURCE OF
PASTORAL LEADERSHIP

As you contemplate growing a soul winning church, you must pause for a moment to examine the man who leads the church.

Many pastors have tried earnestly, even desperately, to have a soul winning church. Most did not succeed. If they did succeed, it was only to a small degree, and for only a short period of time.

There is a *source* of leadership for the task of growing an evangelistic church. There is one significant key that unlocks this whole problem. It is the touchstone of the Christian ministry.

Before we discuss the secret source of pastoral leadership, let us ask this question: why have so many tried and failed? Is there perhaps something in your own life that may stand between you and, not only a soul winning church, but also a *spiritual* church.

This question is far more important than we might at first realize.

I once heard one of the greatest soul winning pastors in America have this question put to him in the presence of a small group of men. His answer was thus:

"The difference between the pastor who does not have a soul winning church, despite all his efforts, and the pastor who does have one, is very simple. One man is seeking to grow a great *church*. The other is seeking to grow a great *people*."

Let us begin this chapter by saying that this author does not know why any one man who has earnestly tried to lead his church into a great soul winning experience has not been able to do so. Every man is a different problem unto himself. Certainly our backgrounds differ, as do our training, and our outlook on life. Nonetheless, it is a fascinating question.

Having a soul winning church is basically a spiritual matter. You do not begin with methods. Methods, alone, will not produce a soul winning pastor, nor a soul winning church.

> One pastor was very blunt and candid in saying, "I invited you here for this campaign for one reason: I am too busy to win souls myself. I want you to teach my people to do it, so that I can attend to other matters."

All the methods, training, program, and gimmicks in the world cannot help a pastor with this kind of attitude. But perhaps he was saying openly what many others have dared only to think. The problem remains basically spiritual.

Be assured of this, you can lead your people to become great evangelistic witnesses. Nevertheless, the fact remains that I have never met a great soul winning pastor, but what that man has had an *overwhelming experience with God*. Call it what you want, there first came a climactic moment in his life when God *broke* him. There was a moment when hidden things—fears, complexes, sin, conformity, traditions, acceptance,— were totally obliterated, and he became a free man in Christ. This must happen to you. It can happen to you. It will happen to you if you want it.

You have a promise from God:

> "If you seek me with all your heart, you will find me."

If there wells up within you a spiritual passion that says, "I must win souls if I never do anything else; I must lead my people to win souls, if I never accomplish another thing"; stick with that vision, that burden, that prayer. Seek it like a starving man seeking water, and God will answer you. God does not play games. He is more serious about this matter then we.

But if you simply have a cold, calculated desire to improve methods, to become better established, to grow a bigger church, build a bigger building, to raise a bigger budget, to have the prestige of a successful church, then you can rest assured that with all your labors and agony to achieve; at best, you can only slightly excel, and that only for a brief period of time. And oh, the effort and hard work you'll suffer through, for such pitifully small gains.

God hides Himself from such fleshly attitudes, even when these attitudes are subconscious. Perhaps God eludes a man with such a motive, refusing to give him the gift of soul winning and the success of a soul winning chuch, because God Himself fears the results in that man's life. What a terrifying thought it is to think of a man with such success, but without the deep and overflowing spiritual capacity to contain it. What havoc could be wrought with such unbridled power.

Here, then, are some of the things that have been suggested as problems in the life of a pastor, that are stumbling stones to soul winning in his life, and to the ability to lead his church into soul winning experiences.

The reasons are not my own. This question has been asked of effective soul winners and great soul winning pastors all over the nation. Perhaps one of the answers fits you, and the Holy Spirit will use it to speak to your heart.

1. Theological Problem

An overemphasis on the sovereignty of God in your life can destroy personal evangelism.

This is a problem faced mostly by Christians from an extra strong Calvinistic background. It begins with a simple and sound belief that God is sovereign in all things. Projected too far into the field of evangelism, it will produce a Christian who simply does not believe that he should witness, or at least not witness until someone knocks his door down and the opportunity becomes so evident that there's nothing to do with it *but* to witness.

There is always a reason why a pendulum swings too far in one direction. It is because it had already swung too far in the other direction. Most people who have this idea about the sovereignty of God, have seen a wrong emphasis on soul winning. They have watched the over zealous Christian walking up to a man, grabbing him by the collar, and begin warning him, in no uncertain terms, about hell.

Notice that the man who almost completely refuses to witness, because of his "sovereignty of God concept", does not let this hinder him at all from *preaching* to win souls. Nor does it interfere with the *teacher* who might teach Bible classes through the week for the purpose of winning souls. The sovereignty of God is invoked only at the point of *personal* witnessing . . . at the point of personally bringing a man to a *decision* about Christ.

There is no logic in this.

We must take every possible, conceivable, opportunity to witness. But our witnessing must be done in the Spirit of Jesus Christ. We must press for decision, but not with pressure. We must give every man the opportunity to reject or accept Jesus Christ as Lord and Saviour.

Some of the finest men who believe strongly in the sovereignty of God, are among the greatest and most gentle soul winners in the world today. There is room for belief in the sovereignty of God, yet with a very zealous, daily, effective, soul winning ministry.

2. An Over Emphasis On Liturgy

Some pastors are so concerned in having formality, ritual and liturgy in the church, that they are afraid of an emphasis in soul winning, both in the church and out of it.

At this point, I would like to say that one of the most effective, Spirit-filled Christian men I know is an Episcopalian priest. If your belief in liturgy, formality, ritual, and "worship atmosphere", precludes soul winning, then your belief is just too strong. You stand on ground that cannot be justified.

3. Seminary Training

Here we move into areas which are much more practical and personal. There are many pastors who are Spirit-filled men, and who earnestly seek to have a fruitful Christian life, in their witness, and in the church they pastor. They have not been able to do so, simply because they have never received any effective, workable training in the field. They cannot produce, for the same reason most men cannot sit in the cockpit of a jet passenger liner and fly it. They do not know how. They have not had the training. Expose a man to methods and concepts that work, and he starts winning souls immediately.

4. A Disproportionate Emphasis On Preaching.

Some men feel that they have been "called to preach" to the exclusion of other things. But there is no such thing as a call to preach which excludes personal responsibilities. There is a romantic, cure-all attitude toward "standing up there to preach the Word". Some seem even to feel that a call to preach is an exemption from personal witnessing. There is no doubt that, in the mind of God, He would have every minister of the Gospel, to be a soul winner more than a preacher.

But there is another subtle, hidden attitude among many ministers, more insidious than the attitude that preaching exempts one from soul winning.

There is a growing devotion to the *art* of preaching—that is, men who make a science of preparing and perfecting their messages. Almost all their waking hours are spent searching for sermon material— thinking and talking sermonic ideas. (Some pastors may smile at this, who perhaps are so busy they almost never have time to work on a message.)

Still, many a minister has heard a message so powerfully delivered that, if he had taken it to his own heart personally, it could have transformed his life. Instead of taking it personally, though, he walks away, saying, "That was great; I think *I'll* preach on that next Sunday."

Such a man often becomes so polished that he seems to arrive at a point of pulpit sophistication, and reaches a point of dignity, that precludes the menial tasks of life.

Winning men to Christ is second to *nothing*. No man has a right to preach an evangelistic sermon (he has forfeited that right) who is not going out each week persuading individuals to come to Christ.

Remember, you can be the greatest pulpiteer who ever lived, but no one will be converted, if there are no lost people to hear you. And this situation of diminishing numbers of lost in our services is becoming more acute every year. We are preaching to fewer and fewer lost souls each season. All the power and pulpit polish on earth will not bring them back. You are living in the wrong sociological era for that. It remains for you to go to them.

We hear too many such frivolous conversations as, "Say, that idea will preach", or "That's a good idea for a sermon", when we should be saying, "Excuse me, now, I must go and *practice* what I preach."

Nor will a message ever reach the pinnacle of power and fervor that it could, until it is beat out on the anvil of personally grappling for the precious souls of men.

5. Living An Unnatural Life

The life of a minister is probably more ideally suited for producing ulcers and nervous breakdowns than any other.

Let this author be the first to step forth in sin confession, for I spent two weeks in a hospital in Zurich, Switzerland, while pursuing a theological education there, with my stomach tied in knots because of nervous tension. And at the grand old age of 19, at that! And in the ensuing years, nothing could panic me more than just the thought of a church business meeting, a deacon's meeting, or facing a word of criticism from one of the parishioners.

There are two phases to this inhibiting life of a pastor: your own personality limitations; and the unnatural limitations which you impose on yourself. Both will stagger a man attempting to lead his church into unusual paths of the Christian adventure.

Personality Limitations:

Most of us are not gifted with natural leadership ability; nonetheless, strong leadership ability is absolutely necessary to have a spiritural or a soul winning church. God has said that He uses "the weak things of the world to confound the wise". We can all attest to this!

Most of us can admit to deep inferiority complexes, and moments of real self doubt. Our limitations are great when it comes to dealing with others, commanding respect, operating under pressure, leading a church into uncharted waters, facing opposition, maintaining an optimistic and Christian spirit in the midst of confining tradition, and criticism.

I have observed that a very large number of pastors are suffering from a nervous disorder . . . have had a nervous breakdown, . . . or "are planning to have one, as soon as I can save up enough money to afford it" . . . or else, they have an ulcer. Obviously this is wrong, even though the problem is getting worse every year.

Again, a very large number of pastors are having real, basic family problems, in child discipline and in getting along with the wife. A man who has not found perfect peace in his own heart, and has not the ability to perfect his own Christian home, can never hope to draw up enough reserve to lead his church to become a truly evangelistic and New Testament lighthouse.

Self-Imposed Limitations

Perhaps we learned it in school . . . it's hard to

say when, exactly. Most of us enter college, the seminary, or Bible college, from off the farm, or a small country town, or else we were wide-eyed, shiny-faced kids from the big city. Nor is it easy to say when we began doing it. Usually we start doing it to cover up some personal or spiritual weak spot. And just as often, it is brought on by environment, because everyone else is doing it.

But, somewhere along the way, most all ministers develop a *false piousness*—an artificial "holy glow", or sophisticated reserve.

It can be expressed in so many different ways— in such subtle ways that, often, we don't even realize it.

It may be a deep, resonant voice; or a strange pronunciation of words, such as "Owa Deah Hawvnly Faathu" . . . It may be a solemn (and just a trace of saintly) countenance . . . or reverntly folded hands . . . or a vocabulary of most inspiring cliches and phrases.

Come, now, fellows—own up to it. Or do you really believe you still have that same, natural, untarnished down to earth personality that you had in college!

Such reserve and artificiality of life, which a man feels he is called upon to play almost every waking hour, is a tremendous physical drain. What a limitation, too, in trying to discover your God-ordained potential, when the true personality is covered over with so much pretense.

Soon a minister loses his natural personality, and does not know who or what he is. How hopelessly confined a man gets. What an "unusable" situation to be in.

These actions are often excused on the grounds of, "You can't afford to become too familiar with your people; they will lose respect for you." Perhaps this is true. It need not be true. A man who truly has the power of God upon his life, and who is bearing fruit, can be just as natural with everyone, as he is with his wife and family when they are discussing the grocery list together. And never lose an iota of respect from anyone!

If it has been, or ever becomes, your privilege to fellowship with some of the truly great Christian giants of this generation, you will find them as common as an old shoe. You will note only that they have a *God reference* about them, that is as natural as their breathing. By the way, it can't be imitated.

If ever we are to make an impact on this world for Christ, we are going to have to step out of our self-imposed imprisonment in our ivory towers, and be our natural, normal selves.

That includes dropping a lot of foolish, unholy "holiness", which we put on every Sunday between the hours of eleven and twelve.

One of the greatest sentences uttered on the victorious Christian life goes like this:

"Allow Jesus Christ to live His life in you, through the power of the Holy Spirit— *expressed in your own natural personality* —to the glory of God!"

6. The Pastor And Corporate Guilt

One of the most damaging, yet subtle, problems that has clutched almost every pastor in every evangelistic denomination in America, is a lack of personal guilt over present day problems.

Get a group of ministers around a table, and you can just about predict what they will discuss. They will turn to the problems that are faced in their denominational body. They will analyze the problems, bemoan the failure, and scorn those who would seem to be at fault.

We seem to have arrived at a point where, if we can analyze a problem, discuss it, and then condemn it . . . we are exempt from doing anything about it!!

We somehow feel that we, as individuals, because we are not "up there at headquarters", are in no way responsible. Or if it is a church problem, we generalize, making it a "churches everywhere" affair— "everyone seems to be . . .", "Christians just will not . . ."

We must come to a moment in our lives when we actually relenquish our concern about our denomination, or the "mess our country is in", or "the way Christians are today", and look at our own lives and our own area of responsibility.

You *are* your denomination. You are the Christianity of this day. You are the moral, spiritual, political problem of this hour. And I am too!

Draw a circle around your own life. Stop looking at the problems around you. Stop looking over the other fellow's shoulder, going "tut-tut". Begin to be an answer. Start creating solutions. It makes no difference if no one else has ever done it. If it will eliminate a problem and glorify Jesus, do it! This is a revolutionary day. We need some revolutionary answers and some revolutionary men. *You* are going to have to be the answer.

For instance, there is a great deal of talk today about the fact that we don't give enough attention to new Christians. We are not properly training them for the Christian life. Then stop analyzing the failure. Create a whole new approach, and put it into effect in your church. Forget about the disease which may be denominational wide, or involve all of Christendom. Work out a solution and put it into action in your church; and while doing it, be creative. Do it in a radical new, workable way.

If you do, rather than being burned at the stake by others for your unorthodoxy, as you might fear, they just might beat a thankful path to your door to adopt what you have done.

We need some old-fashioned, individual guilt and

responsibility for the mammoth problems we face today.

Perhaps you are saying, "but I do not have the authority".

That's just the problem. Not anyone, anywhere, really feels that he has "the authority". Most of the problems we face today are so big and so far out in the ectoplasm, that no one feels that he is solely responsible. We need men who, without being asked to, will tear into the problems of our day, and, as individual men, start coming up with answers! If you wait for the authority to be given you, it will never come. Remember: "The man with the nerve to take the responsibility, will soon be given the authority."

7. Conformity

Here is your main problem. This is the reason we do not have more spiritual Christians. Here is the reason we have almost no soul winning churches.

Mark this: if you ever have a soul winning church, you are going to have to break with tradition. You will *not* have a church that looks like other churches. You will *not* be following the tradition— nor your denominational program of evangelism.

If you ever have a soul winning church, get ready for a personal crisis in your own life. Your life will have to be shattered.

Few men can break with tradition. The Holy Spirit alone can help you through this experience.

You will come out of this experience testifying of "being filled with the Holy Spirit".

The greatest single factor that keeps a pastor from having a soul winning church is *fear*. Fear of breaking with all the conventional concepts, methods, ideas and traditions. Conformity to the *status quo* is our greatest enemy. Throughout the entire Judo-Christian history, tradition and conformity have remained the major stumbling block to spiritual, evangelistic progress.

Perhaps the reason is that none of us thinks we have conformed!

A few years ago, a book appeared entitled, *The Organizational Man.* It traced the fantastic influence of conformity in organizational structure.

It has often been observed that journalism and philosophy, as well as the way we use reason, logic and deduction, are still almost rigidly conformed to the teachings of Aristotle!

The author was recently in Washington, D. C., at the nation's capitol, and heard an address made in Congress that received nationwide coverage. During the next few days, it was my privilege to fellowship with a large number of Christian Congressmen and Senators. I received from them both their reaction, and the reaction of their colleagues about the speech. A few days later, however, I read in TIME and NEWSWEEK magazines, an account of the speech, and what those two magazines reported as being the reaction on Capitol Hill. Both magazines reported the very opposite reaction to the real facts. Yet, those two accounts, written by two journalists, caused literally millions of people unwittingly to conform to the views stated in the magazines.

How often, by TV, newspaper, radio, books, magazines, by teaching, by tradition, and a thousand other invisible pressures, do we unwittingly conform.

The first time you mounted a pulpit to preach, you conformed to 600 years of tradition! When you entered upon your ministerial training, by the very course of study you took, the type of thought pattern, and schedule of subjects you pursued, you conformed to 1400 years of traditional ministerial training!

The only real way to be free from these hidden pressures, is a soul-shattering experience that will make you "free in Christ".

We have already noted that denominational leaders in every denomination are actually wanting—not conformity

. . . but originality. There is no doubt, great men of our day who have grappled with God and searched their souls that they might yield their lives completely to God, will almost always say that the problem of yielding their denominational acceptance, is the hardest of all crises. It is indeed.

Make no mistake, what fellow pastors think is one of the greatest single influences on the actions taken by a minister. We would all deny this. The only way to know how tremendous a problem it is, is to come to a moment when you make a gigantic break with the accepted way of doing things. Then the stark reality of this influence hits you.

There is some fallacious reasoning abroad at this point. There is a widely held view that a man can be only one of two things: "a denominational man", or "a rebel". There seems to be no room for anything between these two stereotypes. This attitude ought not to be. For the most productive servant of God is *neither*.

Both the man who, unbeknown to himself, follows his denomination blindly—and on the opposite extreme, the critic, who seems to be against everything, and proves his "freedom" by the things he fights—both are in a position of *minimum* productivity.

It is possible for a man to be set completely and absolutely free from denominational, traditional patterns—in both mind and soul—and yet still be a man who *never* has a critical word about anything or anyone. That man is his denomination's greatest asset! For he is totally free. He has no fear of conformity, yet his soul is pure. He has a creative mind. He has a fearless spirit; yet he is free of gall. He is actually less critical of his own denomination than those who proudly boast of their denominational loyalty! He is more Christian, and more usable, than the rebel, because there is no bitterness. This kind of man is a rare find in our day, but he is not extinct.

There will have to come a time in our lives when we

yield completely our position, prestige and acceptance. This is not easy to come by. If you do not believe this is your problem, then get up tomorrow morning and start doing everything you believe you should do as a minister. Everything! Start preaching *everything* in the Bible that you believe. Start moving things around in your church and make it everything—yes, everything—you believe a church should be. Begin practicing everything in the New Testament you can find that the apostles did.

Can you?

Yielding "what others will say and think" is undoubtendly the greatest single hurdle to the *Victorious Christian life*, for every minister of the Gospel.

————————

In this chapter, we have examined some of the problems that face a pastor in his own life, as he seeks to grow a spiritual church. What of a solution?

It would seem incredible to believe that there is one solution to all of these many and divergent problems. But there is! As we have previously stated, no man has led his church to become a great evangelistic instrument for God, who himself has not had a crisis experience with the Holy Spirit.

It may have been a quiet moment, when the Spirit-filled life became a clear reality, or it may have been a turbulent thing. But at some time in a man's life, he will have to come to understand and know the fulness of the Holy Spirit.

CHAPTER 11

ENEMIES OF A SOUL WINNING CHURCH

The greatest single stumbling stone to having a soul winning church is, at once, insidious and invisible. Time and again, pastors have confessed that after their church was ignited by a return to personal evangelism, one factor came along to stifle out the fire of revival. It is a problem that must be dealt with. Concrete, lasting solutions must be found, for Satan uses this simple little device as his greatest tool.

The enemy: too much *activity.*

We would do well to review the origin of some of our present day activities, and discover why we are doing many of the things we do.

Almost every present day, church-related, organization was begun for the exclusive purpose of winning souls. This is true of the men's organizations (Brotherhood, Men's Fellowship, Yokemen, etc.). Women's missionary organizations trace their origin back further, and were provoked into existence because of laymen's failure in evangelism. The training unions (training periods previous to Sunday evening services) were started in every denomination, almost exclusively to train Christians to be effective witnesses.

These and other organizations began to flourish, until each found a place in the denomination's departmental structure. Weaknesses and problems arose, so refinements and reorganization set in.

The church stands today, at the close of this century, with almost every evangelical denomination facing an organizational structure so complex that it defies comprehension. Without doubt, this is the number ONE problem facing the average church today.

We begin with a complicated and exhaustive program in the local church. Then this complexity is duplicated by the denomination with sister churches in the vicinity. Then comes the sectional level; the state; and the nationwide activities of the denomination.

All of this organization and activity was started with the thought in mind of producing a greater soul winning movement. But through long years of growth, it has evolved to the point that it is the greatest single *hindrance* to that goal.

Look at the average church calendar:

>Wednesday night—mid week prayer service, and teachers meeting
>
>Monday or Friday night—men's meeting
>
>Monday or Tuesday—choir, or committee meetings
>
>Saturday evening—youth activities
>
>Monday or Thursday—planning meetings; organizational meetings
>
>Other Nights—Bible study, rallies, conferences, planning meetings, and more committees.

Every church activity vies for the Christian's time. The church is actually in competition with the denominational-wide schedules.

In a very large and influential church in Louisiana, the author was leading a Campaign in Personal Evangelism. We spent a whole day with the entire church staff, trying to work out the weekly (and annual) calendar of church activities. At the end of the day, a very final and decisive conclusion was drawn: there was no place possible to work into the schedule any program of soul winning, or even visitation. And there the matter rested!

What is such a fantastic complexity of activities doing to the Christian family?

THE TYPICAL CHRISTIAN FAMILY

The wife belongs to the women's organization. That organization normally has a dozen committees (each committee must meet at least once a month to achieve certain standards). Dozens of jobs grow out of this: records to keep, reports to make, conferences to attend, books to read —just to carry out the mechanics, and keep abreast of the structural set-up.

The husband faces the same schedule in the men's organization. There are meals to enjoy, rallies to attend, messages to thrill, a men's choir, conferences, reports, etc. And all of these meetings call for dozens of committee meetings to bring these big events into being.

The husband and wife attend everything they can together, at the church. We all know that greater personal dedication in a Christian's life always means more church jobs.

No one ever succeeds in being overlooked, when the committees are appointed, such as: grounds committee; maintenance committee; financial committee; building committee; and then there is the *sinum bonum* of all committees: The Committee On Committees!!

Every person in a Christian family belongs to the Sunday School, so there is the year-round schedule of class parties and department parties (and it takes committees, and planning and work to have these), as well as regular class committees!

There are one or two evangelistic campaigns yearly, with preceding weeks of thorough preparation (more planning and committees, such as meals committee; publicity committees; entertainment committee; prayer committees, etc.)

There are also other week-long activities. Christians face a very real and damaging "guilt complex" in trying to attend these special meetings. Credit is usually given if the person has a perfect attendance record. Christians often feel they are being unfaithful to Jesus Christ if they miss—though physical or domestic problems would often dictate the wisdom of spending some time at home.

This is only the beginning.

Almost all loyal church members find themselves in several positions of denominational responsibility. Again, the Christian faces a round of perhaps six to ten denominational organizations meeting in his area every month. With these comes more planning meetings and committees. Included in this are printing; mimeographing; phone calls; travel from church to church and city to city; letters to be written, letters folded, letters stamped, letters mailed, letters read and answered!

There is more.

Usually, there will be at least one important statewide meeting per month that all laymen and pastors are urged to attend. Once again, the whole, involved process is duplicated.

On top of this is the great denomination-wide program, with its annual gatherings. They must carry the burden of truly important commissions, of missions, finance, long range planning, etc. This, with denominational headquarters, has a vast overall structure with multitudes of facets and intricacies.

Each of these departments has leaders and a paid staff. These men are in these positions to produce results. They cannot produce results, without training Christians to be proficient in that particular field; and so a great mammoth flood of meetings, training conferences, and committees and activities are planned.

Christians have never been successful in being Christians and nothing else. There is constant pressure upon the entire Christian family. The community desperately needs Christian influence. There is the PTA, school meetings, an important civic meeting or banquet. Friends come over; there is a birthday party (myraids of them). There are interdenominational movements that call for Christians' participation. There are such things as the March of Dimes or similar benevolent drives; or a political rally.

On top of this, there are school activities—inter-school and intramural—baseball, football, basketball, band concerts, dinners, recitals, socials, etc. Christians are asked to attend these—all of them! You can't say *no* to everything!

For the husband, there are the inevitable responsibilities that come with a job. Besides a rushing hour spent getting to work, eight hours of work, and an hour getting home again, there are overtime, special training meetings, conferences, union or board meetings, office or factory parties. Pressures from friends to join bowling leagues, baseball teams, etc.

The wife is faced with duplicate problems, plus ten hours a day of hard work. She is wife and mother, and president of a large company: the highly mechanized household!

The average husband needs eight hours per week to attend to nothing but maintenance of home, appliances and automobile.

Suffice it to say, the average Christian family is expected to be at some church or denominational gathering virtually *every* night. Christians have to have some of this pressure taken off of them. They have no time to themselves. They are not superhuman. They need rest. They need time alone. They need to be creative. There are a multitude of other things that must be done. As one layman put it:

> "There comes the time in the life of every
> Christian, when he's got to take a bath!"

Any Christian *family* needs at least two nights away from the church—if for nothing else, to avoid a complete physical breakdown.

Someone will justify all these activities, by saying, "If they weren't at church, they would be somewhere else. They wouldn't stay home." Well, glory! Maybe they would go to a precinct meeting and change the political atmosphere that has been created in our land, because the unregenerated are all that are left to run things. Maybe they would go to a PTA meeting, and put a stop to the immorality that is rampant in our public schools.

If what we have said is true for the layman, it is one hundred fold more true for the pastor. It is not uncommon for a pastor to go 100 days without a night at home.

> Never, never, did God intend the Christian
> ministry to come to this!

WHAT ARE THE RESULTS OF OUR ACTIVITY?

What are the results of this "activities orgy"? Here are but a few of the cruel consequences of this problem.

1. Administrative ministers.
2. Physically exhausted Christians
3. A terribly neglected spiritual life
4. No Christian home life
5. A materialistic society almost void of Christian penetration
6. A fleshly church and denominational program, done by sweat rather than by the Spirit.
7. Constantly being hearers of the Word, and not doers.
8. The Christians and the minister completely out of personal touch with the world and the people about them.
9. A church program—and an evangelistic program —that is carried on totally within the walls of the church building.
10. A concept that Christianity and church attendance are one and the same, and that church attendance *is* spiritual depth.
11. A loss of a sense of direction. A Christian spreading his interests over a large field of things must quickly pass on to the next, without ever coming to grips and being victorious in any area.

THE EFFECT ON EVANGELISM

The length and breadth of Christendom has felt the effect of our overactivity. The author has noticed that this is true even on the mission field. The church's program there often duplicates the organizations that we have here at home. Soon the simple native is suffering the consequence of our hyper-tense world.

The results in our churches are predictable and pathetic. Take the exhaustion of almost every Christian, add to that the terror he feels toward visitation (much less soul winning), and you can guess what will be the *first* thing he will drop from his schedule!! Yet, soul winning is one of the few bed-rock, Bible-based activities that a modern church *should* carry on.

VISITATION CANNOT BE MAINTAINED when it is being crowded and competed with, by the multiplicity of organizations and activities.

TAKE YOUR CHOICE:

To have both a soul winning church and a church brimming with activities is impossible. Exhausted Christians will never recognize the Biblical importance of soul winning and visitation, when it is sandwiched in between other activities, and *treated as though it were on the same level of importance.*

Christians will always drop visitation *first*, under the circumstances. A soul winning church is doomed before it is ever started.

If you want your people to engage in New Testament soul winning, then there is no alternative: MANY OTHER TIME-DEMANDING ACTIVITIES MUST BE DROPPED.

WHAT CAN BE DONE?

In the last chapter, we saw that a pastor must face a crisis in his own life to have a truly spiritual church. He must face, with this, the problem of conforming. Right here is one of the testing grounds of victory over the natural urge to conform.

You face a major decision—one of no small consequence, and one that some men never bring themselves to. Nonetheless, winning men to Christ is the greatest single job of the church. Everything else, in God's bookkeeping, is secondary.

The solution: *less* organization; *less* meetings.

(Note: not "none", but "less".)

Someone has said, "If the 20th century church doesn't

simplify its program and get down to cases, there won't be a 21st century church!"

As you begin cutting out activities, you will discover your people are ready to support you. The 20th century layman is ready to revolt at this problem already. Virtually every thinking Christian in America is—layman or pastor! Then why so much activity if every one is against it? Because vicious cycles are always hard to stop.

It's your job to break this cycle. The first step is the pastor's personal experience with God. Whether this experience comes through hours of agonizing prayer and fasting, or through simple commitment . . . it will begin at the throne of God. You will need God's help to face this Goliath.

Here are some suggestions on how to begin:

Lead Your People Into A Soul Winning Experience.

Bore a big hole in your church's calendar. Have a great spiritual drive in personal evangelism, as presented in the next section of this book. Let your people see what they—what the church—can do through personal evangelism.

Then face them with the facts: this cannot continue—it is irrevocably bound to be smothered out, on the treadmill of activities, unless these activities are curtailed. Your people will know by then what happens in their own lives when the church building becomes a battle station, and the church itself goes to the lost!

Tell your people honestly what must be done. Ask their cooperation. Get their positive suggestions. Talk it over with every organization. You will be amazed at the response.

THEN:

Present A Plan.

Start with a principle, such as this:

"Everyone should have four nights at home. That means the church will be open three nights each week."

From this principle (four nights per week or three nights per week) work out a plan. Ask the men to meet only once a month for their organization. Ask the ladies' organizations to meet only once a month too. (Go ahead; you've got nothing to lose— except perhaps your head!)

Solidify Committees; Eliminate Committees.

Eliminate non-productive organization. Cut down on parties. Change them from monthly or quarterly, to yearly affairs, and major on quality instead of quantity. Raise the standards of a few, basic meetings.

As pastor, resign gracefully from a multitude of other activities.

Exert stronger personal leadership. Learn the art of being a leader without being a dictator; strong without being unkind; firm without being dogmatic.

Think originally! Ask every activity: "Where did you come from?" "Why are you still here?" "Are you really productive?" "Can you be cut down, cut out, or changed to become something better?"*

Have A Family Night.

Once or twice a month, you can make your midweek service an "All Church Activities Night", and on the other weeks have a regular Wednesday evening prayer or Bible study service. This allows all church activities to meet . . . all at the same time, without adding another night to the church calendar.

It can be done.

To have a soul winning church, IT MUST BE DONE!

---

* One pastor moved mid-week prayer meeting to Tuesday, and Visitation to Thursday. That gave the members every other night at home. Though this may not work for your church, it illustrates originality. Another pastor began personally teaching all the Sunday School teachers on Wednesday evening in a meeting just before prayer service. He began formulating and passing on plans and programs to them; they in turn passed the news to the rest of the church, through their classes. The church became unified under one source; and many activities, committees, etc., were eliminated. (Quality of teaching also rose!)

CHAPTER 12

THE MECHANICS OF A VISITATION PROGRAM

Reaching his arm far back into the bottom drawer of his desk, the Educational Director said, "*Here* are our prospect cards. I knew they were somewhere around here!"

This is similar to misplacing the engine of an airplane.

The importance of the *mechanics* of visitation is often overlooked by church leaders. Very little is to be had in this field in our Bible schools and seminaries. Precious little has been written on the subject. Conclusive research is almost non-existent.

Poor procedure in a visitation program can, and always will, completely demoralize those who attend the visitation program.

Unfortunately, the situation described above is far too typical. So perhaps it would be easiest to understand the problems and the principles in the mechanics of visitation by looking at a typical church today. As we do, we can learn how *not* to have a visitation program.

A LOOK AT A TYPICAL CHURCH

It is "Visitation Day" at the church. Let's see what's going on:

In the typical church, those who are going visiting come straggling in at odd times. A few will get there on time, but most will be coming in from five to thirty minutes late. There is talking and laughing. There is no particular place to sit or to meet. Everyone just stands around. The pastor may be there; he may not be.

Often the visitation cards are not in a box, but are hanging on a "Visitation Board". Each worker goes to the board or to the box and picks up the cards of prospects he wants to visit. There may be a prayer; there may not be. Rarely will there be any specific instructions.

What happens after they leave the church is even more pitiful. Some will leave, taking only one card. Others will go with a whole handful of cards. Some will go out to visit alone; others will go in threes and fours. Usually, they will forget to have prayer in the car.

The situation worsens as they arrive at a home. Some will go to a home to find out that the person listed on the card moved away two years ago. Others will find the addresses wrong, or the information incorrect. Some of the workers will be met at the door by such comments as, "We had three visits from your church last week". The worker will look at the card and see that none of these visits were recorded on the card he has.

Someone else might say, "We have already joined another church and are active in it; and we have already told several other visitors from your church to please not come back." Again, there would be no such information on the visitation card. Others will knock on the door to be met by this comment: "Oh, a couple from your church was here just a few minutes ago to visit my daughter." Duplication in visits abounds.

What happens when visitation is over?

Some will come back to the church just a few minutes after departing, making the comment, "Didn't find anyone at home". Others will be out for several hours. Tragically, many will not even return, but go to their own homes instead; taking their cards with them. Those Christians who do not return to the church rarely ever return their cards either, and the church loses any knowledge of the visit and its results.

The prospect cards get lost by the hundreds.

Those who do return to the church after visitation is over, often fail to report their visit on the back of the card, and many of those who do report their visit do not write a good clear account of the visit.

This kind of visitation program is doomed to die. There is no way it can survive. Yet, it is typical of most churches today! It has within itself the seeds of its own destruction. There is too much uncertainty, too much chaos, too little discipline, complete lack of direction. Information is inaccurate. Almost everything about such a program leads to complete destruction. Soon the number of workers will drop off and after not too many weeks, the visitation program will die.

Can this pitiful scene be changed?

Yes, it is possible to solve all the major problems you face in the procedure of a visitation program. Following is a list of the key problems involved, and the principles you must introduce to solve them.

I.

HAVE A "VISITATION SERVICE"

You have a morning worship service every Sunday morning. The people do not stagger in all through the service, walk around, leave at odd times. You begin at a certain time, and follow an order of service.

This is what visitation must have. It must have discipline. It must begin at a certain moment. Each week everyone should know exactly what to do. They must all come in on time, get their cards at a certain time, and leave at a certain time.

In Chapter 23, an "Order of Visitation" is suggested. Briefly: you begin *on time*, with a song, a prayer . . . then a word of instruction. Then the pastor hands out the cards. Everyone promptly leaves — going in two's, with a definite time to return.

Never let the workers select their own cards.

Some churches make the mistake of having a "Visitation Board", with prospect cards hanging from nails, for Christians to come by and pick them off at random. Other churches mail visitation cards out for Christians to use "sometime during the week". Neither of these ideas will *ever* work, effectively. Not until the inertia of human nature changes.

You must have a definite time set aside, when everyone in the church comes together for the one expressed purpose of visiting. The meeting must be conducted with as much discipline as a Sunday morning worship service.

II.

PREPARE FOR VISITATION

When Christians come to the church to get prospect assignment cards and go visiting, they come to work for God. They mean business. When they get there and the cards are not ready for them, and there is delay and confusion, and a general atmosphere of disorderliness, and the pastor and others fumble through cards—the seeds of destruction are being sown.

The pastor needs to arrive early and have all the cards picked out, stacked in order, and ready to be handed out instantly. This is one of the greatest *single* answers for a successful visitation program.

III

USE A FAMILY PROSPECT CARD

There is one thing we can know for certain in any visitation program: AN INDIVIDUAL ASSIGNMENT CARD *WILL NOT WORK*. The only effective way to keep your prospect file and make assignments is with a family card.

If you make a visitation card for each individual, you will have at least *four* times as many cards to keep up with (and lose).

When you send a couple out to visit using an *Individual* prospect card, *it is possible that three or four couples may visit the same home the same evening*.

What a waste—a duplication of energies. What a way to make enemies . . . no one can receive four visits from *one* church in *one* evening without getting a little irritated! And what a way to demoralize Christians out visiting.

Furthermore, there is no way to keep accurate visitation records. One card, on Mrs. Brown, may be *blank* on the reverse side. This would indicate that no one has ever visited that home. But eight visits may have been paid to Mr. Brown . . . all dutifully recorded on the reverse side of his card. There is no way to know this when looking at *Mrs.* Brown's card.

A family card eliminates duplicate visits, and the record of visits that is kept on the reverse side gives a "historical record" of all the visits to that family.

THE STORY OF A CARD

Just about every Christian education director has invented a prospect card at one time or another! And where is there a pastor who cannot show off his own card design!

Some five years ago, I began to talk with pastors about what needed to be included to make an effective prospect card and file system. We analyzed dozens of cards—all that we could locate — gleaning the strong points from each. This undertaking alone took a number of months.

Here were our conclusions.

We needed a card which could be arranged (all at the same time!):

> geographically—preferably by streets
>
> by age
>
> by sex
>
> by *type* of prospect (membership or unsaved)

It *had* to be a family card, but one that *individual assignments could* be made from! At first glance, that looked impossible. It needed to be big enough for space on the back of the card to record as many as six visits.

If possible, all this needed to be made available to the pastor by simply opening the box and looking at the cards, without moving them. It also needed to be (!) simple.

(We wanted to avoid a rainbow array of different colored cards, and different colored tabs.)

Schemes to achieve these goals were myriad. There were card colors, tab colors, different size cards. Name it. Truthfully, though, only the inventors could ever hope to figure out the systems. We also tried something that holds fascination for everyone, the *punch card!* This is a card' with a hundred holes around the outer edge. By taking a rod (like an ice pick), and poking it through the holes, you can pick up certain types of cards. It sounds great, and many have tried it. But it is still a good idea only if you have a $20,000 machine to do all the complicated sorting and re-sorting for you. Like gasoline made from water —it is a great idea, but it just won't work!

We talked our problem over with some men from IBM. After analyzing their suggestions, and taking a clue from an Addressograph system, we discovered that a *scaled* tabulation system solved all the problems. There were no color schemes. Instead, the position of the tab told the whole story. (Tabs are placed at certain positions on a scale printed at the top of the card.) By just looking at the place where the tab is, you see everything.

Each tab on the card represents *one* member of the family. There will be *one* tab on the card for *each* member of the family. The position of the tab tells both the *age, sex,* and *type* of prospect. The cards are placed into the box by streets. The family name is also conspicuously printed near the top of the card. All this information could be "seen", without moving the cards. The card was 5"x9", which fits into a regular 6"x9" file box.[1]

This prospect card went through about five revisions in the experimental, mimeographed stage, and then over 15 revisions in the *printed* stage! Over a quarter of a million of these cards were in print, and then recently, it was picked up and adopted by several of the nation's largest denominations.

In the following chapters, we will present a step by step plan for the whole field of visitation and for personal

---

[1]By agreement with the author, the Gospel Publishing House has prepared a Census Card similar to the author's. The card, reproduced on pages 248 and 249, may be ordered in quantity from the Gospel Publishing House, Springfield, Missouri 65802. The card number is 7-5330.

evangelism. The basic principles are discussed here in this chapter. These principles, again, are:

How to keep from losing prospect cards.

Eliminating duplicate visits to a home.

Visitation reports as historical records.

Keeping a record of *every* house in your community.

Individual assignments from a *family* card.

One last word about cards. Often a pastor attempts to set up a card system by *zones*. He assigns "zone captains" whose duty it is to visit in that zone, and keep the pastor posted on anything important that he discovers. Zones are artificial, and will never really be understood clearly by anyone but the pastor. Better to make all assignments by *streets*. Besides, the zone captain idea will work effectively for *only* a few weeks. It is impossible to designate responsibility to a large number of volunteers on any such project, and expect good results from everyone, on a permanent basis!

Losing Cards — Visitation's Biggest Problem

The most destructive problem in visitation is the loss of cards. More important, is the loss of the *record of visits*, which is on the back of these cards. The record of past visits to the home of an unsaved man is as valuable as any records a church shall ever have! The author has been in many churches throughout the nation that had a full-time secretary whose job was to do nothing but type and retype duplicate prospect cards. This is such a needless waste of human effort.

With a minimum of effort, the loss of cards, and therefore, the loss of the record of visits, can be *totally* eliminated. You need not even bother to make duplicate cards.

Prospect cards are just as sacred and valuable as the church's membership roll, business minutes, and financial records. (None of these is duplicated. Rather, they are kept under lock and key for safety.)

Our whole attitude toward prospect cards must change.

A prospect card is an HISTORICAL DOCUMENT. It is the history of a church's relationship to a home, a family, and to immortal souls!

There is another reason that prospect cards need to be treated in a new light. When a new pastor moves to a field, he knows nothing about what has gone on before. He knows nothing of the people, their needs, or what has been done to help any of them. He looks at the prospect file in vain. Cards are outdated. The cards he sees, tell him no story of past visits, give no hint of the true status of the prospects. They are too outdated; they have been duplicated and re-worked too many times; and too many other cards are forever lost.

Seeing this pathetic situation, the new pastor takes a census. A visitation program is started. The pastor begins meeting people, visiting the lost, and putting together a picture of the community's spiritual life. After a year or two of valuable time wasted (time that need never have been lost, had he inherited adequate records) he finally knows as much as the *former* pastor knew *on the day he moved from the church!*

The new pastor learns no lessons from the former pastor's mistakes. Most of the knowledge of the community is now in this pastor's head—not on cards. When he moves, he will probably also leave inadequate records. The process begins anew.

If a new pastor could begin with a prospect card file which recorded in detail the last five or six visits the church had made to *every* home in the community, he could begin the *first day* where the last pastor left off.

This is only logical. We do this with all other church records, such as our financial records and church membership records. We must do it with the *most important* records of all. Prospect cards *are* HISTORICAL DOCUMENTS!

Most pastors have given up, as a lost cause, any hope of ever training their people to be better stewards of their cards. To envision a day when *no cards* are ever lost, is beyond the realm of faith.

Really, though, the solution is simple. Here is a principle: begin by having one day a week for visitation. Make the handing out of cards a very orderly, disciplined affair. Insist that *all* cards be brought back right after visitation is over. *Never* let the cards out of the box on *any other day* of the week. Never let anyone have cards unless they can return their cards immediately after they finish visiting.

You can inaugurate this simple principle during the Week of Visitation (see Chapter 22). Your people will get used to the new routine.*

As one educational director reported to me: "This program works so well that only *one* person ever loses cards any more." I asked why he didn't stop that one person, and he replied with a twinkle in his eye, "because he's the pastor!"

You can expect to have results *at least* that good!

WHERE TO LOOK FOR PROSPECTS

There are two kinds of prospects.

First, there is the

EVANGELISTIC PROSPECT.

The evangelistic prospect is the person who is not a Christian. He may be a church member, he may not be, but he is lost.

Then there is the

MEMBERSHIP PROSPECT.

This is the person who is a member of your denomination, and lives in your community, but has not moved his membership into a local church as yet.

---

* A detailed plan on how to carry this out is discussed in the chapter entitled "The Weekly Visitation Program".

There are four ways, or places, to locate these prospects:

> from the Sunday School Roll
>
> Sunday Visitors (visitors who fill out a card when they visit your church)
>
> The Newcomers List
>
> The Religious Census

Let's take a look at these two kinds of prospects and the problems they present. Then let's take a look at the *four* ways to discover prospects and see the problems there.

As we do, keep in mind that the purpose of your church is to locate *every* lost person in your entire community, and witness to him personally about Jesus Christ.

The Church Membership Prospect:

It is not the purpose of this book to show you how to get church members to join your church. Nor is it the purpose of this book to show you how to reclaim "backsliders".

Let me make one observation: I have found that I can win to Christ and enlist 25 unsaved people for every one backslider that can be reclaimed. (The reason may be the one D. L. Moody gave: "the thing that's wrong with most backsliders is they've never slid forward.")

We must stop—dead, cold *stop*—thinking of all church members as Christians. They are not. As this book unfolds, you will learn a way to find out whether church members are lost or saved. You should seek to find this fact out about *every* person in your community who is a church member.

The Evangelistic Prospect:

Very few people today admit they are *not* church members. Even fewer admit they are *not* Christians. As you attempt to locate prospects, a whole new approach to this problem must be used; otherwise, you will discover few evangelistic prospects in your community.

Now, let's take a look at the four sources of prospects. Most churches lean heavily on the first two: the Sunday visitors and the Sunday School roll. But the *best* and largest source of prospects is from the last two: the Newcomers List and the Census.

1. The Visitors Cards:

The people most frequently visited by Christians are those who have paid a visit to the church, and signed a visitors card. Tragically, but truthfully, in almost every church in America, the pastor does not even have enough Christians out for visitation to visit *all* of the Sunday visitors.

Many churches have long since settled down to a visitation program that *never* reaches beyond this group. The thought of having a program that could reach an *entire* community would be sheer incredulity.

The typical church is certainly a far cry from the great soul winning church we mentioned in an earlier chapter: that visits *every* newcomer moving into the city of over a million, (where there are several thousand newcomers per week). It can be done!

2. The Sunday School Roll:

The other most frequently used source of prospects is the list of unconverted people who have been enlisted into Bible classes.

The great bulk of visiting done by churches today is to this group, but the visits are made on the wrong level.

These prospects are often visited dozens of times . . . with only an invitation to "come to Sunday School". If an evangelistic invitation is sounded, it is secondary to the enlistment invitation.

These "Sunday School prospects" are zealously visited over and over again, but the Christian always says, "Come to Sunday School"; never "Come to Christ". The human heart being what it is, the prospect just will not respond. He is being approached on the wrong level of human need and human interest. A form of "Gospel hardness" sets in. (Really, it is "enlistment hardness".) As stated before, the appeal of the church to a lost person is zero.

I have found, contrary to all stated rules, that these lost people who have been visited so very, very much—in an attempt to get them enlisted in Sunday School—are often *not* the easiest to win to Christ. On the contrary, they have set up a "negative barrier", and are frequently the most difficult of all to reach.

The easiest person to win to Christ is just the very average American citizen. He sits around home in the evenings; he *never* goes to church or Sunday School; and has not worn out his vocal chords saying "No" to enlistment efforts. He has a lonely heart and a plaguing little notion in the back of his head, that he needs Jesus Christ. When *correctly* approached about his need of Jesus Christ, he responds. Thereafter, he makes a wonderful Sunday School and church member—*without* being begged!

In at least 80 per cent of the churches I have observed first hand, the evangelistic prospects were being taken from only two sources—Sunday visitors and the Sunday School roll. Rarely ever has this list been over 200 names, at a maximum. This is a long, long way from the New Testament vision of taking a world for Christ.

The result of this lack of vision is appalling. The average church does not seem to be able to see the miles and miles of houses around it. These houses seem to lose their true meaning to us. These houses actually represent thousands and thousands of people who need Jesus Christ. Usually, a church sees the community only from the other end of the telescope —as though there were only a microscopic number of lost people in the community.

Many times a pastor has mentioned the small number of prospects that his church has. When asked about the myriads of homes in the community, he often responds: "Most of them go to other churches."

Ah, but there is hardly a community in America where over 20 per cent of the people are in church on Sunday morning!

Almost all the families in your community are prospects! You can see them as prospects when they are looked upon with the correct vision (the Acts 20:20 vision)!

Nor do most of us see the terrible limitations we have placed on ourselves and our church, by having so *few* prospects. A pastor who proudly boasts of 200 prospects, rarely realizes he is actually limiting his church to a maximum growth of a few dozen people.

We spent the entire day in one church (which had an attendance of over 700) looking for evangelistic prospects. At the end of a day's work of going through every file in the church, we had located the names of only 25 prospects. By every law of evangelism known to man, that church could not hope to win *over* 10 people to Christ in the next year.

(That was exactly how many they had won the year before—ten.) This was a church with an annual budget of over $150,000 per year, and with six full time staff workers!

Now let us take a look at the other two sources of prospects and see what problems and opportunities they afford.

3. The Religious Census

The third source of prospects is the Religious Census. When a new pastor moves to a church, one of his first actions is usually to have a religious census. The average pastor in America stays in a church less than three years. Most pastors take a religious census soon after coming to a new field, so consequently, most churches have a census about once every three years. Most churches are working from a religious census that is outdated.

In the past we have looked at a census as designed to do two things: (1) locate the lost; and (2) locate church membership (or denominational) prospects who may be living in the community.

The religious census is usually very effective in locating church membership prospects. For locating the lost, the religious census has almost always been a failure (though we rarely recognize it as being such).

This is not intended to be a statistic, but the author has checked the results of scores of religious surveys. In most cases, less than *five* per cent of the people surveyed will admit that they are "not church members" or "not Christians". Of course, more people than that are unchurched, and certainly more than that are unsaved, in any community.

We must begin to realize that we live in a nation where "everyone is a church member", and everyone thinks he is a Christian. This is one of the most crucial problems facing 20th century Christianity. We must find a whole new principle by which to approach this problem.

To do so the Religious Census must be revolutionized.

A church can usually expect a religious census to produce these results:

About 50 per cent of the houses will be surveyed.

While 50 per cent of the houses are missed.

The information received on the cards is usually so sketchy that the cards are of no real value.

Often many members of the families are not listed on the card.

The age of each person is not listed, which renders the rest of the information almost meaningless.

Addresses are incorrect, and information on each person is scanty.

Worst of all, though, nearly half the homes are never contacted.

All of this must be changed if we are to reach *every* home, and every person in *all* the community, for Christ.*

4. The Newcomers List

The Newcomers List is one of the most valuable sources of prospects. It is the one and only key to *continued* church growth. Newcomers to a community present the *greatest* single *evangelistic* opportunity you have.

A church that will: (1) take a religious census; (2) make that census 100 per cent complete and 100 per cent accurate; (3) inaugurate a strong visitation program; and (4) couple this with a Newcomers List . . . can keep a prospect card file up to date and accurate INDEFINITELY.

The Newcomers List is about the most important single necessity to locating evangelistic prospects. It is just about indispensable.

You will have to begin using a Newcomers List, if you are not presently doing so.

You can find out how to get the Newcomers List, by calling the Chamber of Commerce. (Also, look under "Welcome Wagon" and "Newcomers" in the telephone directory.)

Such a list is available in every town and city in America. (In the towns or cities in America where no *official* list is kept, contact the funeral homes, or

---

* One entire chapter is given over to step-by-step instructions on how to take a Religious Census. A plan is presented to solve these problems.

some door-to-door sales agency. There is always a list available somewhere.) *

For a clear understanding of the problems that face you, and the principles that will solve these problems, we have presented this chapter. In the remainder of this book you will see a plan unfold that can eliminate these death-dealing problems which have destroyed so many evangelistic programs.

Someone has said, "The real solution to any problem on earth is always a simple solution." You will find the unfolding solutions to be very plain, without gimmicks, but a simple, workable program which can be used without alteration, year after year.

---

*Rural communities excepted.

CHAPTER 13

A NEW CONCEPT IN SOUL WINNING METHODS

Can a quiet, reserved, timid Christian become a soul winner? Is it possible for the *average* Christian to be transformed into a soul winner who is as effective as the best?

In this chapter, we will seek to introduce a whole new concept in soul winning methods. As far as this author knows, it is the first time the principles, philosophy and science of this new method have ever been presented. It is the author's conviction that this very new—yet very old— approach has proven to be the most effective method for winning men to Christ developed in modern times. It has not only produced more soul winners; it has produced more *effective* soul winners than any concept in the past 200 years.

In beginning, the author would like to take a moment to speak, not with the pastor, but with the theologian who might pick up this book. Until now, this new concept has been received almost unanimously by everyone who has come to understand it. As it becomes better known, it is bound, by all the laws of history, to fall under criticism. May I say this to you, before you pick up your first stone of criticism: please do not tear this house down unless you can, and do, build a better one. If you can find a better, and more New Testament, approach to soul winning, then you will have rendered mankind one of its greatest services.

Also, if you have something to say, earn the right to say it by being an effective soul winner yourself. All the theological reasoning (of which this author is totally in-capable) may be very profound, and sound very correct; but is the man who speaks a personal evangelist? Until you are, you have not earned the right to speak on the subject.

Please, sir, until these two qualifications are fulfilled, hold back your stones.

THE LOST CONCEPT

We have overlooked the one greatest principle in witnessing. This oversight has kept soul winning from becoming a natural part of the Christian's life. The principle is this:

In order to be an effective soul winner, YOU MUST LEARN TO WORK WITH THE HOLY SPIRIT.

Without realizing it, we have built our past methods of soul winning on a concept that almost completely leaves out the Holy Spirit.

Let us illustrate this. In almost every book written on soul winning, under the chapter title, "How To Begin", we are told simply to begin the conversation by asking: "Are you a Christian?" or, "Are you saved?" or, "Do you know Jesus Christ as your personal Saviour?"

Is this working with the Holy Spirit?

Let's say a Christian is sitting with an unsaved man, and turns to him and asks, "Are you saved?" The question falls out of the sky, blunt and piercing. How long has the would-be soul winner actually given the Holy Spirit to work on the heart of the man he is speaking to? How much time has the Holy Spirit had to prepare him for such a direct, blunt question?

Not even a second.

The lost man is jarred by such an abrupt beginning. The Holy Spirit has not a chance to prepare the man's heart. The results are almost always disastrous. Furthermore, most Christians are totally incapable of being so aggressive.

Let us look at the ministry of Jesus Christ. Even He found it necessary to work with the Holy Spirit. We see this very vividly in His soul winning conversation with the woman at the well. He did not start the conversation by bluntly saying, "Are you born again?" or "Are you going to heaven?" He began very slowly, giving the Holy Spirit time to prepare her heart and convict her of her needs.

In our own vernacular, He actually said, "May I have

a glass of water?" From that point on, He gradually moved the conversation from a mild spiritual plateau, very slowly raised it to a conversation about eternal life, and finally drew her to Himself. He gave the Holy Spirit plenty of time to do His office work of conviction. What if Jesus had started the conversation with his *final* sentence ("The one you are speaking about is the very one talking to you now"), rather than His first sentence ("Give me a drink"). Why, He would have frightened her speechless.

It is impossible to witness effectively unless you give the Holy Spirit opportunity to prepare the heart.

It is also interesting to note that the Samaritan woman presented many arguments and excuses during the course of their conversation. Jesus—unlike us—has not answered one of those questions yet! Rather, He guided the conversation around them, and always moved to a higher spiritual plane of thought.

What about Nicodemus, though?

It would seem obvious that Jesus was not working with the Holy Spirit when he spoke to Nicodemus. Nicodemus knocks on the door and walks in. Without even a greeting, Jesus faces Nicodemus with this statement: "Ye must be born again."

How abrupt!

What is the difference in the way Jesus witnessed to Nicodemus, and with the woman at the well?

The difference is this: the Holy Spirit had already prepared the heart of Nicodemus. He was probably already very disturbed and convicted. This is the reason he came to Jesus.

On the other hand, the Samaritan woman had probably not had a spiritual thought in *months*. She was totally unconcerned about her soul. Had Jesus been so abrupt with her, He would have had exactly the same results we do when we are abrupt. She would have thrown up a barrier that would have been impenetrable. Jesus was not so unwise.

We need to ask this question: are most people like Nicodemus, or like the woman at the well? How many people have come knocking at your door, asking you to show them how to find Christ as Saviour? This will not happen to us more than once or twice in a lifetime. Most people are like the woman at the well. They have not had a spiritual thought in months! Approach them abruptly, and you will never reach them. Begin the conversation gradually, as Jesus did, and amazingly, these very difficult people actually become very easy to deal with.

The secret: working with the Holy Spirit.

I.

BEGINNING THE CONVERSATION WITH A LOST PERSON

What are the problems that you face when beginning a conversation with someone you want to lead to Christ?

The *first* problem is that the Christian is "scared to death".

This is the major problem in personal evangelism. It transcends all the long list of qualifications, of do's and don'ts, listed in most books (such as, know the Word; have compassion; memorize Scripture; be soul conscious; live a clean life; etc.) It is not these myriads of things we list that keep Christians from being soul winners. The fact of the matter is, the average Christian in an evangelical church today desires desperately to be a soul winner. It is simply because Christians do not know how to win souls. This lack of knowledge produces fear. The methods they have used in the past have gotten them in such terrible situations that they have abandoned the idea of soul winning.

Soul winning is, without doubt, the most terrifying thought of a Christian's life. Wonderfully, though, when a Christian learns to work with the Holy Spirit, he will no longer have the problem of fear. He can witness with the calmness he knows in ordinary conversation.

The *second* major problem is *resentment* on the part of those you try to talk to. Why all this resistance? Because the Christian does not know how to *begin* witnessing properly. Most Christians finally come to the point in the conversation where they know they must *begin* witnessing, and without any preparatory remarks to pad the shock, will blurt out: "Are you saved?"

Let us take the viewpoint of the lost person for a moment. Most of us have convinced ourselves that all lost people are hardened, resentful, and antagonistic to witnessing. Nothing could be farther from the truth. But when a lost person is approached in this abrupt manner, his fleshly nature rebels. He throws up a "defense mechanism"—a barrier. Almost scornfully, he looks back as if to say, "Well, buddy, I'm just as good as you are." Immediately, we get the impression that he and all lost people are extremely hard to deal with, and have no desire to be approached on the subject of eternal life.

The fact of the matter is, we have simply failed because we are witnessing in the power of the flesh, without the assistance of the Holy Spirit.

The *third* problem we face as we begin a conversation with a man, is that we always get a "Yes-I-am-a-Christian" answer when we ask. Nine times out of ten, he will say, "Yes, I am a Christian." I remember very vividly sitting in the home of a man who had a fifth of whiskey in his hand, and while pouring himself a drink, leaned back with an air of righteousness, and said, "Why certainly (gulp) I'm a Christian"!

We will never find out if a man is a Christian by asking him. Virtually everyone will say "yes". Furthermore, they are honest. Most people have no idea if they are saved or lost. Later on in this chapter, we will learn an entirely different way to find out if a man is really a Christian. There is a way to find out if a man is a Christian, without asking him. He will tell you if he is a Christian, without ever knowing he told you!

Now, let us look at the situation as we have it. Two

men are talking. One is trying to witness to the other. The Christian is scared; the other man is angry. The Christian can't find out if the man is really lost or not. What a situation. No wonder most of us have not been able to win souls!

What is the solution?

Working with the Holy Spirit!

HERE'S HOW:

Begin the conversation on a mild plane. Meet the lost man on the level he is on, not on the level where you want him to be. If he is a disinterested person, then you must never start at the point of maximum conflict (ie., "Are you saved?")

Begin gradually, and the Holy Spirit will create interest in his heart. Gradually build the conversation—letting the Holy Spirit prepare the man's heart with one sentence, so that he is ready to accept another sentence just a little more personal—then another. Finally, after the Holy Spirit has used each sentence to prepare the way for the next, you will be able to ask an all-important question, which, if it had been asked in the beginning, would have produced terrible tension between the two of you.

You will be amazed to discover how well the Holy Spirit has done His work. The lost man will be ready to receive the question, and no tension is experienced at all.

You see, if a Christian can begin *slowly* as he moves into this personal area of a man's life, then the Christian will not be frightened. The lost man, since he has not been slapped in the face with a direct question, begins conversing with the Christian on a very mild spiritual topic. He relaxes. He has no fear that the Christian is going to "pressure him into something". The lost man gains confidence in the soul winner. The two people soon become quite natural and relaxed in their conversation. The lost person will "open up", and begin talking about things he perhaps has rarely ever discussed before. He will not become angry. The conversation will gradually, and very naturally, move toward deeper spiritual levels.

Remove the problem of fear on the part of the Christian, and resentment on the part of the lost person—and you have solved the major problems in soul winning.

1. How To Begin A Conversation Gradually.

It is truly wonderful to see how the Holy Spirit prepares a heart when a Christian is witnessing with a prescribed objective in mind. The Christian always knows exactly where he is going. He is never at a loss. By asking mild questions in the beginning, the Christian gives the Holy Spirit time to stir conviction. By listening carefully, he also learns a great deal about the lost person. The lost person is unconsciously forced to keep his attention on a spiritual topic. Such a concentration on a spiritual topic gives the Holy Spirit fertile ground for working.

The Christian may begin a soul winning conversation something like this:

"Bill, how long have you lived here?"

("About two years.")

"Well, since you moved here, have you and your wife given much thought to spiritual things?"

The Christian waits for an answer. Bill might say, "yes we have", or he might say, "no, we haven't". The Christian can move on to the next question in a perfectly relaxed atmosphere, and with the lost person's interest just barely pricked.

(Each question can be so worded that regardless of the answer, the Christian can move on to the next question. In this way, the Christian *always* knows what to do next. He never has to face into a "great unknown" when he witnesses.)

The Christian can then say,

"Bill, what would you say is a person's greatest spiritual need?"

The lost person will put forth an answer of "Going to church, I guess", or "Praying", or he will say, "I don't know".

The Christian, quite naturally, moves to his next question. The conversation is moving just a little more toward the main point.

"Have you ever heard of the four spiritual laws?"

Of course, Bill will answer "no". The Christian has introduced a thought that just barely stirs the curiosity. The Christian can then say,

"These are the spiritual laws that govern our life and our eternal destiny. Has there ever been a time in your life when you thought about your need of eternal life?"*

Notice: you, the soul winner, are introducing the terms that are being used in the conversation. You are introducing the thoughts. You are guiding the conversation. The lost person will quite naturally pick up your terms and begin to use them in his answers. Here again, you have given the Holy Spirit an opportunity to work, for each time he uses these thoughts and terms, their meaning burns deeper into his conscience.

We have worn out such terms as "lost", "saved", "born again", "are you a Christian". The terms used in this "gradual" approach are all relatively fresh. The lost person is neither offended by them, nor does he realize exactly where the conversation is leading. Therefore, he is relaxed in his replies.

II. How To Find Out If A Person Is A Christian

About the fourth or fifth question, depending upon how well the lost person is responding, there comes the most important question of all.

---

* The lost man may answer, "yes, I have". This obviously tells you two things: he is not a Christian, but he is interested. If he says "no", then you have still learned that he is not a Christian. (If he should answer "I think I have already done this, the Christian can still naturally move on to the next step.) The next question fits naturally.

At this point, we want to introduce a concept that can revolutionize evangelism. It answers the question, "How can you really find out whether a man is converted or not?"

In the chapter on the Religious Census, we point out the fact that many denominations today no longer stress the need of salvation. Your neighborhood is literally filled with lost church members (most of whom have not been to church in years). It should be your goal, and the goal of your church, to visit in the home of every one of these inactive church members. It is not your job to pass judgment on them before you go. We must never make the mistake of assuming these people are saved; nor should we make the mistake of assuming they are lost. Your job is to visit the home to find out which is true. Christians go to a home to make a *discovery*.

We must find out if people are truly born again, or truly lost—without asking the question. (Because the question gets a "yes" answer from nearly everyone.) Then we can throw open a whole new avenue of witnessing.

For one thing, we can begin working in the greatest unevangelized field on earth: the *lost church members*. The evangelistically minded church can quadruple its prospects when it can find out who is lost and who is converted. Too, lost church members need Jesus Christ as much as anyone.

How can this be done? It is very simple:

Instead of asking a man if he is a Christian, ask him what *he thinks* a Christian is. Here is an almost infallible law: *if you can find out what a man thinks he has to do to become a Christian, you will find out if he is a Christian*. Let's turn that around. Find out what a man thinks he has to do to get to heaven, and you will find out if he is saved or not.

There is one thing a born-again child of God

knows, if he doesn't know anything else: he knows he didn't become a Christian by living a good life.

You may ask this question: "Bill, in your opinion, what would you say a person has to do to be a Christian?" (or, "to get to heaven").

For some reason, lost people enjoy answering this question. They will often lean back and say, "Well, sir, I'll tell you what I believe. If a man will live a good life, pay his debts, and do the best he can, he'll get to heaven." This is the depraved thinking of a lost, legalistic mind. A child of grace can never make such a statement. You can know for certain that this man, no matter how religious he may be, has never had an experience of salvation.

This is the question you want to train your Christians to ask in every home they visit in. (The answers they get should be recorded on the back of the prospect's card.)

The next step the Christian takes is all important. When a man gives the wrong answer, it will be the natural impulse of the Christian to say, "No, that's wrong." Many Christians make this mistake, even after they have been trained over and over not to. It is imperative to *never* disagree with a lost person when asking this question. Otherwise you might end up in an argument. So when a man says, "I believe that all you have to do to be a Christian is live a good life, and obey the Ten Commandments", the Christian should answer agreeably,

> "You are right; a person does need to live a good life. But what does a person have to do to become a Christian?"

The Christian can then ask,

> "Could we take three or four verses of Scripture and see exactly what God's Word says about this?"

If you have moved very slowly and given the Holy

Spirit an opportunity to create interest, he will allow you to read the Scriptures. (If he will not let you, then there is nothing more you can do. The Word of God is the criteria for all soul winning. Out of thousands of interviews, I have personally had only four people to ever refuse to let me read the Scriptures with them.)

In summing up, begin the conversation with the lost person, *slowly*. This is just as effective as taking weeks to create an acquaintance with him. The Holy Spirit will prepare his heart for more pointed questions. On about the fifth move upward, ask him his opinion about what a man has to do to become a Christian. This will tell you if he is lost or saved. If he is lost, ask for permission to read some Scriptures, and see what God's Word has to say on the subject.

II.

PRESENTING CHRIST

In almost every book written on soul winning, the largest part of it is given over to discussing ways to answer excuses and arguments. At this writing, the author knows of only three books in print in the English language, that are exceptions to this rule.

In most books, you are taught to ask a man if he is a Christian. If he says "no", and if you are one of the few brave people who had the courage to get past this frightening question, you will then run into a barrage of excuses, such as: "There are too many hypocrites in the church"; "I am just as good as anybody else"; "I will get around to it someday", etc.

All of us have been taught dozens of Scriptures to give as answers to the lost person's excuses.

Here, again, we run up against the fantastic neglect of working with the Holy Spirit. Answering excuses is the greatest error we could make. The moment we begin answering a man's excuses, or even allow the conversation to get down on a level where the excuses are brought up, we automatically have allowed *him* to set the standards of the conversation.

Answering a man's excuses and arguments has absolutely nothing to do with witnessing. It is not even in the same category. This is not witnessing; it is a debate. The Christian is then actually in the role of defending Christianity. Answering specific problems is not, and cannot be, the Gospel of the Lord Jesus Christ! We have never been commissioned to analyze theological points with lost men. We are to present the Good News!

When we realize this, then we can approach soul winning from an entirely new vantage point. You will discover that there is actually a way to witness without having to answer arguments or excuses. Instead of having to answer excuses, the excuses are never brought up. The very nature of the conversation eliminates them. Here again is the power of the Holy Spirit.

Let me reitterate, that never in my entire life have I seen anyone fall under deep conviction from having someone quote a host of Scripture verses in reply to a host of excuses*.

Giving logical, reasonable answers to his theological questions also nets no results. Nor do I know of any truly effective, consistent soul winner who uses that method. (There are some soul winners who have even written books teaching this method, and they themselves never use it.)

In the New Testament, you will find a *great deal* of Scripture proof-text, in *sermons*. You will find virtually none in the personal conversations of a Christian witnessing to the unconverted. The only times that Jesus used the Scriptural proof text method for answering arguments, was when He encountered the devil, and the religious pharisees—never with the sinner who needed a Saviour.

---

* Scripture memory and witnessing are two separate phases of the Christian's life. Scripture memory serves as a wonderful and valuable tool to personal Christian growth.

When we use verses of Scripture to answer excuses and arguments, we are actually magnifying problems, rather than magnifying Christ. All attention has been focused on a very low spiritual plane. More than this, we have already lost before we've gotten started, because we have cut across one of the greatest traits of human nature: *A man will never admit that he is wrong.*

None of us ever really loses an argument. No matter what the subject is, we will do everything in our power to prove that we are right. We will draw upon all our resources, throw our keenest logic and reasoning into play. When we have exhausted facts and logic, we will begin inventing them! When this is depleted, we may resort to just plain lying! From then on, it is no longer a logical argument; emotions are brought in, and we are soon dealing in personalities. Any husband and wife who have ever been in an argument with each other should understand this.

Here is one of the reasons that we have completely misconstrued the interest of lost people in salvation. We have wrongly concluded that most unconverted people are antagonistic; do not believe the Bible; do not believe in God, etc. This is not true at all. All these crude arguments we hear from lost people do not really reflect their hearts. The lost person is only bringing up these points in a desperate effort to win his argument. Once he has taken the opposite position from yours, he'll do anything, bring up anything, say anything, just to win. Tragically, it is *our* fault the conversation takes such a turn.

Let's retrace a typical conversation between a Christian and a lost person:

The lost person says there are too many hypocrites in the church. The moment we turn to a verse of Scripture, we unwittingly challenge him to an argument. We have taken the opposing view. The battle line is drawn. (The battle is lost before it is even started.) The lost man will do everything in his power to prove his point. Logic is pitted against logic, and when this is exhausted, the conversation may very well degenerate to a level in which the lost person is saying things he never believed at any moment in his life. Finally, emotion enters into the picture, and what started out with the highest resolve to witness, ends up being nothing more than a spat.

And where is the Holy Spirit? We have given Him absolutely no place to operate. We have built the witness on a fallacious principle. For the Word of God says the *natural* man perceives not the things of the Spirit. And here we are, arguing theology with the *natural* man.

What are the spiritual principles of working with the Holy Spirit in winning souls?

First, Jesus said that He sent the Holy Spirit into the world to convict the world of sin. This transforms witnessing. It is not your job to convict a man. Pelleting him with a long series of verses showing the sinfulness of sin, to get him under conviction, is *not* Biblical. The Holy Spirit convicts, *not* you!

A doctor does not pound on a man's stomach to prove that he has appendicitis. He merely touches it. The patient will flinch because the problem is already there. It is the Holy Spirit's job, not ours, to produce conviction of sin. You need only make the truth clear. The Holy Spirit uses the avenue of truth that you have made available to Him. He convicts.

Secondly, the Word of God does not say, "If verses, and proof texts, and arguments be lifted up, they will draw all men to Jesus." Rather, Jesus said,

"And I, if I be lifted up from the earth,
will draw all men unto me."

(John 12:32)

Here is the secret to witnessing — Present Jesus Christ.

We will learn in this chapter that there is a way to so present Jesus Christ, and to so present salvation, that this, in itself, eliminates arguments and excuses. Problems are never brought up. This is not a forced, mechanical thing that deliberately sidesteps issues. The opposite is true: the disappearance of difficulties is the natural result of *effective* witnessing.

Finally, we can look at this from the viewpoint of reason. Most of us as Christians are very timid. Jesus has already promised that He will use the weak things of the world to confound the wise. Most of us are not good at memorizing Scriptures, and under pressure, cannot call them to mind. Most of us cannot win an argument through logic and reasoning. All our lives, we have come out the loser in arguments.

And tragically, in witnessing, even if a Christian has a keen memory and a sharp edge of logic, he may win the argument, but rarely does he win the man.

III.

HOW TO ELIMINATE THE PROBLEM OF EXCUSES

You eliminate the problem of excuses, by simply presenting Jesus Christ as Saviour. This can be done in such a unique way that an excuse or argument looks out of place. Here is a part of a dialogue from a soul winning plan employing this new concept.

The Christian is talking:

> "In Romans 3:23, we read that all have sinned and come short of the glory of God. This simply means that I am a sinner; it means that everyone in the world has sinned. You realize you have sinned too, don't you Bill?" ("Yes.") "But most of us don't realize how serious it is when we sin. We look about us and compare ourselves with others. For instance, you look at me and say, 'Well, he does a lot of things I wouldn't do'. Or you might say, 'There is a man over there who is very religious, but I am about as good as he is'.

> "Now, Bill, as long as I compare myself with you, and you compare yourself with me, we never really

see sin for what it is. But God does not compare us with one another, as we do. God compares us with Jesus Christ. Bill, if the Lord Jesus were standing right here, and God were to compare you with Him, would you be able to say you are as good and perfect as Jesus?"

("No, of course not.")

"And, neither could I. No one can. None of us is as good as Christ. But God says if you are not as good as He is, you are a sinner and eternally separated from Him."*

Now, let us analyze this dialogue, and see how it completely eliminates excuses and arguments on the part of the lost person. Notice that *you* bring up the excuse. Then you introduce Jesus Christ and relate the excuse to Him. Rather than answering the excuse, you place the man in his correct position with Jesus Christ. This itself produces conviction and totally *eliminates* the excuse.

Here is a very practical and helpful principle: if you know what a man's excuses are, then bring them up *before* he brings them up. That way, sides are never taken, and no opportunity is given for argument. (Here is something else you might keep in mind: if a man brings up an excuse or argument, never try to answer it at that moment, for this is the moment of greatest tension, and he is ready to defend his position at all cost. Rather, wait and discuss his argument several minutes later, when it is no longer a pressing issue.)

Something more important than this is present in the dialogue, though. It is the PERSON of Jesus Christ. You have told the lost person exactly what most people say. Then you lift the conversation completely out of the realm of the carnal, out of the realm of excuses and arguments,

---

* This point is made very lovingly and kindly. The soul winner goes on to present the results of sin, and then how Jesus Christ has made a way of salvation from sin. Then the Christian clearly shows exactly how to receive Christ as Saviour.
The entire conversation is centered upon the Person of Jesus Christ.

out of the realm of theological debate. You lift it up to a realm in which he is helpless—for you introduce the Person of Jesus Christ. You have asked him, "If Jesus were standing right here, could you say you are as good as *He* is?" Ah, this is a place where the Holy Spirit can operate. The lost person has had to see himself, as compared with Jesus Christ. He will never come back and say to you, "I am as good as anyone else". To bring up such a trite issue becomes wholly out of place, for he has had to stand face to face with Jesus. And the Holy Spirit has brought home the message.

Now to answer a very practical question: "What do you do if someone brings up an excuse in the middle of your witnessing?"

Let us answer this first, by saying that once a Christian learns how to work with the Holy Spirit, and make Jesus Christ the center of the message, this almost never happens. For most of us who have used this concept, it is hard to remember the last time someone has been difficult to deal with. It is rare indeed when a person brings up an argument or excuse. This does not mean that many do not reject Christ. Many do, but never with the agonizing problems and tension we used to experience. Nor does it mean that the Christian so dominates the conversation that the lost person can't get a word in. To the contrary, the lost person usually does the greatest part of the talking. The Christian just guides the trend of thought.

If the person does present an argument or excuse while you are talking with him about Christ, you can do one of two things:

First, be honest and admit your ignorance. If we were to be truly honest, most all of us would say "I don't know." Never make the mistake of trying to give an answer to everything a man brings up. Don't think you are duty bound to try to give an answer to everything. You don't have to know all the answers to be a soul winner. We simply don't have that many real answers. You can be truthful with amazing results. Who said we had to sound like intellects to witness! Nor does the lost person expect you to be a genius, in order to qualify to talk to him. Rather, he will probably respect you more for honestly saying you don't know the answer to his question.

Secondly, you can ask for the privilege of putting the question off, by simply saying, "I'll tell you what; let's go on, and in a moment, we'll come back to that question." Or you can say, "Let's wait just a moment and I think we'll see the answer to that question real clearly."

The very fact that you do not answer the excuse will mean more to the lost person than if you did. He will sense in you an honest and simple desire to present something to him that seems very important to you, and something that you sincerely believe. He will sense that you have come to speak with him about something that is far too important to be pulled down to the level of an argument or defense.

Does this mean that we are never to answer a man's argument or excuse? That is exactly what it means. This desire to quote Scripture to answer a man's every word, will lead nowhere. Still, the soul winner must ask God for wisdom to know the difference between an *excuse* and a *sincere problem*. The difference is really very easy to recognize. If there is something in the mind of the lost person that keeps recurring, then you may be able to tell that this is a problem, not an excuse. Analyze the question. Was it asked humbly and sincerely, from a heart that seems to be wrestling with a problem; or is it asked with a tinge of self righteousness or unconcern?

Ask yourself this question: is the Holy Spirit dealing with the person I am talking to? If you see evidence that this question is borne out of unrest, induced by the working of the Holy Spirit, then very tenderly, do your best to answer the problem, keeping Jesus Christ as the central thought. If you do not know the answer, simply, honestly admit it, and leave it to the Holy Spirit to overrule the problem. (You will find that people with a very serious problem, needing special guidance, will make up a *very small* percentage of the people you talk to. Most people have many excuses, few real problems.

By employing this concept in soul winning, you will never need over four or five verses of Scripture to witness to anyone. Four verses of Scripture can be very simply mastered. They are not four verses which answer four excuses. In a very real way, they are not four verses at all, but four parts of *one* picture — the picture of salvation. They fit together as a whole, to lift up Jesus Christ as the answer to man's need.

Each one of us is very different. Our personalities are never alike. But here is a New Testament concept in personal soul winning that can be, and is, acceptable to the personality of every Christian. Even the most reserved, sensitive Christians, who would be repelled at the thought of witnessing by most methods, find this to be so natural that they can accept it and use it naturally every day.

Once you have mastered these New Testament principles of witnessing, and eliminated the traditional efforts at witnessing, you will be amazed to find how truly interested most people are in Jesus Christ and His salvation. More and more, you will find your conversation getting into the heart and soul of that man's every day problems and needs — such as peace, worry and frustration.

You will be amazed to find that most people are eager to find Christ as their Saviour, when you approach them in the right way. You will discover that it is a very simple matter to win them to your Saviour. You will also discover that it is not such a terrifying experience after all.

IV.

THE POINT OF DECISION

When you witness to someone, the conversation falls into three natural divisions: (1) beginning the conversation; (2) presenting Christ; (3) the moment of decision.

On the shelves of my library, are most of the books written in the English language on soul winning. In hardly a one of these books can you find so much as a reference to the way to carry a man through the experience of conversion. The most that is said is usually, "now press for a decision." Or "now draw the net." But how?

The author remembers vividly, after he had been a pastor for three years, and had completed the seminary, that he was talking to a lost man who suddenly agreed to accept Christ right then and there. Although I had witnessed to dozens of people, up to that moment, not one of them had ever showed any interest in accepting Christ (nor had I ever succeeded in winning any of them)! It was only at this moment, that I realized that I did not have the vaguest notion how to carry a person through a salvation experience. I believe that this has been typical of most of us. We do not know how to lead a lost person through the experience of salvation.

Most pastors and laymen have never received any training in, and know nothing about the very sensitive art of pressing for a decision. About the only way to draw the net that most of us have ever heard of is for a Christian to say to the lost person, "If you will receive Christ as your Saviour, put your hand in mine."

But man's hand does not save! The decision must be more conclusive than this! Certainly prayer does not save; nonetheless, a lost man must some way come in contact with Jesus Christ to be converted. The absolute minimum for anyone to receive salvation—regardless of what a man knows or doesn't know about redemption—is that he must come in contact with the Saviour. Prayer does not save . . . but Jesus does; and a man has to come in contact with Jesus to be converted.

The greatest tragedy of soul winning today, is that we never get around to explaining, step by step, exactly HOW to receive Christ, and then LEAD the lost person through these steps. I have watched Christians deal with lost people for hours and yet never get around to saying: "Here's How".

Furthermore, there is no such thing as *witnessing*, if a

point of decision is not reached. Most Christians have concluded that if they invite someone to church, or say something about Jesus, or even present the redemption story, then they have "witnessed". A man has not truly witnessed until he has brought a soul face to face with Jesus Christ, to the point where that man must either accept Him or reject Him.

The most effective, and yet the most gentle way to come to a point of decision, is to simply present the plan of salvation, and then, without wavering or even slowing down, ask him to bow his head with you while you have a word of prayer. Request that he close his eyes and imagine that Jesus Christ is standing there. Pray a very brief prayer, and *do not close the prayer*. Just stop talking to Jesus, and start talking to the person under conviction.

Say to him:

> "Now, Bill, don't do this unless you really want to, with all your heart. But if you would like to receive Christ as your Saviour, right now, just say, 'Dear Lord Jesus, I confess my sins . . .'"

Then wait for him to begin praying. He now knows exactly what to do, and how to do it. You have brought him to a clear point where he must knowingly reject or accept Christ.

He will often begin praying, and pour out his heart to the Lord without your assistance. Or you may need to guide him through a complete prayer of decision.

After you have led a man to Jesus Christ, your very next words should be on assurance of salvation, and then his need of becoming a part of the church, and growing in Christ.

GUIDING THE CONVERSATION

We have looked at the problems and the principles of effective New Testament witnessing. When a Christian has thoroughly mastered the art of soul winning, then he almost completely loses his fear of witnessing. Witnessing becomes a daily experience — and it is done on the highest level of Christian virtue. Witnessing becomes a glory to Jesus because the way it is done *glorifies* Him. This begins a new day in the life of a Christian, and also in the life of his church.

A Christian witnessing effectively can actually guide the conversation, if he is master of what he is doing. The lost person may talk a great deal, and should. In the beginning of the soul winning conversation, when you are moving slowly, you should let the lost person do most of the talking. The Christian should encourage him to talk, by listening attentively, and perhaps nodding. But the Christian sits there knowing exactly what to do next.

He knows exactly where he is headed. If the conversation veers off, he can bring it back immediately. After all, a conversation is simply the interaction of words and ideas. It is possible for the Christian to guide that conversation gently, up to the point of opening God's Word, and from there, into the truths of salvation — skillfully moving in the opposite direction of excuses — and finally leading the person to the point of decision.

THE BEGINNER NEEDS A PLAN

It is possible to reduce the principles which we have discovered and talked about in this chapter, into a workable plan. This plan is simply a dialogue. The Christian learns five or six "approach steps" that can gently and slowly open a conversation with a lost person. These six steps quietly lead that person up to the point of opening the Word of God with him. One of these questions the Christian asks will reveal if the person is truly converted or not. Each question is so worded that, regardless of the answer the lost person gives, the Christian can ALWAYS move on to the next question. In this way, he is never at a loss as to what to say next.

The Christian can learn a dialogue, which explains clearly the plan of salvation. He uses four verses of Scripture which clearly present Jesus Christ and moves the conversation to a point of decision.

The best way for a beginner to win souls is to master ONE plan. All of us are beginners, so it would be best if we all started here. Master and memorize the plan as if it were the only one in the world that would work.

Here are some reasons why a Christian seeking to be a soul winner should use a plan:

1. It gives you confidence.

2. You have the advantage of knowing what reactions and responses to expect from your prospects.

3. Your mind is free of the stress of planning moves, leaving you free to concentrate on your prospect, and the Lord's presence.

4. You can guide the conversation.

5. It allows you to stay on the target, and work systematically toward your subject's salvation.

6. It leaves you free to analyze the prospect's answers and responses, and measure his understanding. You are not desperately wondering what to say next.

7. You do not need a lot of Scripture verses or extra helps for the job.

8. You can bring your man to a decision faster.

9. You, yourself, do not become confused.

10. The lost person develops confidence in you, because you reveal confidence.

11. You do not have to annoy yourself with "How will I bring up the matter of Christ and salvation?" Memorized approach steps make it simple. Fright disappears.

12. You will always be ready when the Holy Spirit gives you an opportunity.

13. You are relaxed and natural. There is no fear at all.

Use the plan you have mastered, until you have successfully led about ten people to Jesus Christ. By the time you have won ten people to Christ, you should be completely over the problem of fear. Also, you will have sat under the greatest soul winning Instructor on earth—the Holy Spirit. You will have a backlog of experience on which to draw. You can cut your ties with the plan, and witness out of the overflow of wisdom that God has given you . . . by any approach you deem best.

Until the time when you graduate from the beginner stage, you should stick with the plan.

This is the best way for a pastor to begin soul winning in his own life. It is the best way for the pastor, in turn, to *teach* the art of soul winning to his people. It is the best way for a layman to begin winning souls to Christ. It is the best way to begin building a soul winning church.

CHAPTER 14

A NEW CONCEPT IN SOUL WINNING TRAINING*

Soul winning cannot be taught in one night. It can't be taught in three nights. It cannot be taught at all. It has to be individually mastered. Soul winning is a sensitive art. It is an exacting science, filled with pressure and crises. It should never be taught lightly. It should never be studied briefly.

Learning to be a soul winner boils down to hard work! The only effective way to teach or learn this art is by using every teaching concept there is. Mostly, it calls for group participation and practice. A Christian should continue in study until he has mastered his subject completely. To send a group of Christians out to witness before that point is reached, will be almost disastrous.

You will need a minimum of 5 to 7 sessions (about 1½ hours each) to thoroughly saturate Christians in their curriculum, and turn them out as real *artisans*, to witness. Here is one of the places in the Christian life where you just have to settle down on one point and go over and over it, until finally you have mastered it. Have you ever realized that we rarely give such concentration to any part of the Christian life? We touch on everything, flee to something else, but never stop to become specialists at anything.

WHAT METHODS WILL BE USED?

There are several methods of teaching that may find an important place in soul winning training, such as lecture, motion pictures, phonograph records, charts, etc.

Still, the key to soul winning is for the Christian to *see* what he should do, and then *practice* what he has seen, until it is second nature with him.

---

* This chapter is to be studied in connection with the chapter entitled "The Week of Training"

We have already discussed the need of teaching a *plan* to our church members. That plan will consist of:

(1) Beginning — the (six) approach steps

(2) Presenting Christ — using four verses

(3) The point of decision

You will also want to teach:

How the church visitation program is conducted
The art of visiting in a home.

HOW NOT TO TEACH SOUL WINNING

Most instruction on "how to witness" has been delivered in *lecture* form. Learning to play the piano by attending lectures would net about the same results!

Others often employ a "skit", drama, or pantomime. These offer some visual help, but a great many of the audience's questions are left unanswered and there is no opportunity to practice and master what has been seen.

The audience must be brought into the act! Confidence cannot possibly come to a Christian until he has conquered the fear of the unknown, by trying it himself.

The best method of teaching, is a cross between lecture, demonstration, and discussion! This can be best understood by illustration:

Let's say you are the teacher. You should be standing on a stage *without* a large pulpit, so that your actions can be seen from head to foot.

Let's imagine you are teaching the art of visiting, and want to show the audience what to do at the door: how to get into the home; what to do when you get in.

First, quickly review the entire situation which you are about to demonstrate. Explain the problems that will be confronted. Then draw a word picture of the scene. Point to where each part of the scene is located.

Now act out a very small part of the scene. (You must be part "ham", to teach soul winning effectively.) You might demonstrate getting out of the car and going up the steps. But at the same time, you must pause to talk to the audience about different aspects of what is happening. For instance, tell them to look about the yard to learn something about the family — while you are doing the demonstration.

Then knock on the door. Stop. Turn to your audience and explain that there are three or four things that can happen when the door opens. Dramatize one of them. Stop. Turn to the audience, make any necessary observations, then call for questions from the audience. Then illustrate the *second* thing that might happen at the door. Repeat the process.

You continue this each step of the way, talking, acting out details of the action and the visit, inch by inch . . . then stopping to explain again . . . then calling for questions.

Tell exactly what to do after getting into the home. Then act it out. Then stop. Talk about it. Then call for discussion. Also, and most important, break into demonstration and have the audience to practice saying the things they have seen you do and heard you say. (Have the audience repeat aloud several times, exactly what they are to say when the front door opens.)

You should teach soul winning in this same way. After you have finished explaining, acting out, and discussing, then ask the entire audience to repeat aloud the part of the dialogue which is under discussion. Later, you will have the entire audience split up, scatter out in pairs, and have practice lessons. Having the audience repeat aloud, and then having a practice session, should be continued each night until the entire art of visiting and soul winning has become second nature to everyone.

PRACTICE SESSIONS

The key to mastering the art of soul winning is repetition and practice.

When you begin the training, you should have the audience repeat the (six) approach steps. They should read the four Scriptures aloud, and then perhaps repeat key sentences.

On the second night, you can start the semi-practice. At some point, pair everyone off in two's. Have them all face you and repeat the approach questions aloud. Then, while the questions are still fresh on their minds, have them to practice the questions on one another. After that, have each couple practice reading the verses to one another.

Continue to gradually build the content of the practice sessions until each pair is going through the entire plan with one another. Warn everyone to be fair. The person playing the part of the lost person is just a "dummy". He is not to try to make the situation difficult for the soul winner, but instead, to be very cooperative.

Remember, the purpose of this Week of Training is not to slightly expose Christians to soul winning, but to subject them to an intensified, repetitious, practical, down to earth program of training that will produce highly skilled artisans.

PART III

THE PLAN

CHAPTER 15

INTRODUCING THE CAMPAIGN IN PERSONAL EVANGELISM

ITS ORIGIN AND PURPOSE

How can a church become a great soul winning institution?

How can ordinary — even timid — Christians become the best of soul winners?

How can such results be permanently sustained?

Every pastor has probably dreamed of having laymen who would call him every week telling of people they have witnessed to . . . and won . . . to Christ. Every pastor would like to see new Christians coming into the church —every Sunday—because they were won to Christ in their own living rooms.

Can all this actually come true in your church?

These are awesome questions. The problems of developing an evangelistic church can sometimes look insurmountable. There must be an answer, though. Somewhere, there must be a simple, basic program — without frills or gimmicks — for consistent evangelism. There must be a way that every church can have an effective evangelistic ministry.

When the author first began receiving invitations from fellow pastors to explain to their churches how to visit and win souls, I did not really realize that this was a totally unexplored field, or that there was a whole science of evangelism, waiting to be discovered.

My own church had an overwhelming experience in personal evangelism. Among other reasons, we had introduced some of the discoveries I made while interviewing and studying the programs of the great soul winning churches, and the methods of the world's best soul winners.

Other pastors began asking to have these discoveries shared with their congregations. This was the birth of what was to develop into an exploration of the *Science of Personal Evangelism.*

It began as a simple, one-night discussion on soul winning. The results were often electrifying. The pastor, and perhaps one or two laymen, would often begin leading others to Christ and the church. Sometimes this personal work continued; at other times it did not.

Later, these discussions were extended into a full week. This gave us a chance to explore the art of teaching soul winning in detail. A whole new approach began to emerge. It also became obvious that teaching soul winning without teaching the art of visiting (from a soul winning perspective) was ineffective. Both were then taught together.

In our first meetings we discovered it took at least an *entire week* of training to get Christians ready to win souls. This includes nearly two hours per night for seven nights, in the most practical, down to earth training and practice sessions imaginable, before Christians were finally ready to make an initial effort at visiting and witnessing.

Often both pastor and people have observed that this was the first time in their lives that they actually stuck with one subject until they had completely mastered it. And they knew they had mastered it, too.

In those early meetings, after this very intense Week of Training, the church simply went into a *one* night a week visitation program. It was obvious that the results we were seeing were a phenomenon. No one seemed to have heard of anything comparable.

Still, there was something very basic missing. It was at this point that we really began to research this field earnestly, and ask questions.

Two other ingredients have to be added into this foundation — a foundation upon which a soul winning church can be built. These two steps transformed personal evangelism in the local church. They are the two most essential ingredients of all.

A breakthrough in modern evangelism came when we added intense *spiritual preparation* to the meetings. Suddenly, the meetings began to take on the atmosphere of revival of bygone days. No, that is not right — a revival spirit unlike anything we have ever known! Without any emotional upheavals, without any large gatherings, there was a spirit of individual excitement and spiritual growth. And along with it, the fruits of new babies born into the Kingdom, with new experiences piling up daily, all producing a continuing surge of revival throughout the church and community.

Now after our training sessions were over, the pressure of activities, and the traditional way of doing things was still having its effect. And even after six or eight weeks of brilliant harvest, churches would often gradually creep back into an 1800 year old rut. Something was needed that would produce an explosion in the life of every Christian. The only way to solve this problem was to get the Christian in a position where he would have such an insatiable, unrelenting desire to witness that *these daily pressures would not be able to quench his fire.*

After all, fruit bearing is natural! Soul winning should never be forced. It should come as a natural part of our daily lives. The ultimate purpose of a soul winning church is not to produce a strong visitation program, but to produce Christians who just naturally witness every day. This, alone, is true New Testament evangelism. This is also the purpose of *this* book. Not to show you a method of operation, but to point you to a way that your church can be perennially winning souls. A church that wins souls all the time, does so because there are Christians in the church who just can't stop witnessing.

There is a way to set such a fire in the hearts of Christians.

The answer came in having an entire *week of visiting* to follow the week of training. The results are far more amazing than you would ever think.

No one — not even those who have experienced it — can justly describe what happens to a church, a Christian, and a community, when a body of Christians spends *one solid week* in winning others to Christ. The mental breakthrough on the Christian is a phenomenon. You cannot explain what happens to a Christian who has had to think, eat, sleep, pray, talk, and DO soul winning for six straight days.

A week of witnessing is not at all like one night of visiting. The experience literally breaks in on a Christian's life, and remolds it. At the end of such a week, a Christian is just *not* willing to go back to being an "average" Christian, nor is a church ready to return to being a "normal" church.

This simple procedure on which our soul winning classes were based, gradually refined itself, and later developed into the "Campaign In Personal Evangelism". This is an intensive two-week campaign to get a church *started* toward becoming a great soul winning church. This campaign is the *first step* to take in leading a church to become truly, *naturally*, evangelistic. Behind it is a very New Testament concept: a program to totally evangelize an entire community.

Here are some observations that can be made from these experiences:

1. Laymen are not ready to win souls to Christ unless the training has been unbelievably thorough. It is folly to believe that anyone can go out and win souls after one or two, or even three, nights of training. This will not work. If something besides results is wanted, it's fine. But for producing soul winners, it is totally ineffective.

2. You cannot teach Christians and then send them out, the same evenings. Some churches will try a soul winning emphasis that combines training *and* going every night of the week — thirty minutes of training Monday evening, then an hour of visiting,

and so on through the week. This is like sending a man out to fly an airplane each night after about 30 minutes of instruction. There will be only ONE flight. In both cases, the rest of the week is spent in funeral arrangements!

3. A new approach to soul winning is needed.
Soul winning methods and soul winning instruction must be done in a wholly new dimension. These facts have already been observed in the second section of this book.

4. Another observation can be made:
Personal evangelism, to be effective, and then *lasting*, demands spiritual preparation as intense and thorough as any ever planned for an evangelistic campaign. This is a law of God. Intense spiritual preparation is essential! Very often, a church experiences a great spiritual revival through their *preparation*, for it demands so much prayer and heart searching.

5. So the last observation to be made is this:
In building the foundation for successful soul winning, Christians need to be subject to an intense and *prolonged experience in visiting* and witnessing. This gives everyone *many* opportunities to put into practice what he has learned. It sets up new patterns of thought and action. It breaks down old patterns.

To the layman, the Campaign looks like this: two months of preparation; a week of training; another week of visiting.

For the pastor, it is much more. It is often like going back to school. There are many new areas of evangelism that must be explored. A whole new perspective must be taken. Skill is needed, and the pastor must master all phases of this concept.

There is a real science to church-directed Personal Evangelism. For instance, there must come a whole new attitude toward the Religious Census, the Visitation Service, the Prospect File System (and its correct use).

There is also the SCIENCE OF SUSTAINING EVANGELISM.

It is one thing to get a church doing evangelism. It is another thing to KEEP it going! Both pastors and Christian education directors recognized the acute lack of practical training offered in this field. There is an equal lack of practical, proven material and tools. Nonetheless, mastery in this neglected area is essential.

This is what a Campaign in Personal Evangelism can accomplish in your church. Remember that it is nothing more than *Step One* in having an evangelistic church.

It will:

Train Christians in the art of soul winning.

Give the Christian a prolonged opportunity (through six straight days of visiting) to put into practice what he has learned.

Make the Christian conform to, and become accustomed to, a new kind of church visitation program.

Bring about the conversion of a large number of the unsaved. (You can expect to win as many, or far more, than a regular evangelistic campaign. This depends on the amount of preparation made.)

You will make the entire church "soul conscious", pressing home in powerful ways, the need and the dynamic of soul winning.

It will produce soul winners who will not want to ever stop witnessing.
It is a foundation upon which you can build a permanent, sustained program of evangelistic visitation.

It can possibly bring about a revival in your church — greater, deeper, and more lasting than any your church has ever experienced.

The best possible way for you to develop a soul winning church is to begin with an intensive drive in personal evangelism that touches every area of your church, and all its people. This is the purpose of a Campaign in Personal Evangelism.

Here are the steps you and your church will go through to have a Campaign In Personal Evangelism:

1. The Religious Census and other preparation.
2. Spiritual Preparation
3. A Week of Soul Winning Training
4. A Week of Soul Winning Visiting

What happens after your church has a campaign in Personal Evangelism? How do you *keep* soul winning alive?

The year-round program of evangelism will follow the pattern developed during the Campaign.

After the Campaign is over—and the week of visiting concluded—then the church must quickly move into the program of SUSTAINED EVANGELISM.

SHOULD YOU HAVE AN EVANGELIST TO FOLLOW A CAMPAIGN IN PERSONAL EVANGELISM?

Here is an all important question that must be faced: should you follow this Campaign in Personal Soul Winning with a mass evangelism (ie., revival meeting) campaign. Should an evangelist be invited in to reap the results of such a great undertaking in personal soul winning?

What seems to be the obvious answer . . . is the *wrong* answer.

WHY NOT WORK MASS EVANGELISM AND PERSONAL EVANGELISM TOGETHER?

You must choose between two things if you are considering combining the two kinds of evangelism at the outset of your efforts to have a soul winning church:

Do you want TEMPORARY results, or LASTING results?

A campaign in personal evangelism is designed to do more than win a large number of people in a short length of time. It is designed to give your church a consistent, perennial ingathering of souls.

At first, it would seem logical to combine a mass evangelism campaign and personal evangelism campaign for a great harvest of souls. Every pastor who has sought to produce a great weekly program of evangelism, — but who followed it with "mass evangelism", — *has always regretted it.*

Often, it is said that the greatest evangelism on earth is a combination of mass and personal evangelism. Agreed! But this is just theory. We *have* mass evangelism. We do *not* have personal evangelism. It exists largely, at this time, as a theory. We will never have personal evangelism if we continually confine all our efforts to producing it in just a few weeks of activity before the coming of an evangelist.

In the beginning, when you first seriously set out to create soul winning in your church, you must isolate personal evangelism from mass evangelism, enlistment evangelism, and everything else, and concentrate on the accomplishment and mastery of this *one* goal.

To try to harness personal evangelism and mass evangelism, at the very outset of your efforts to grow a soul winning church, is futile. This is like trying to work a flea and an elephant together. As soon as you grow the soul winning talents of your church up to the size of the elephant, *then* harness them up together. NOT until then!

A Campaign in Personal Evangelism is executed for the purpose of concentrating the efforts of Christians on soul winning for a long period of time. The very first thing to do after the Campaign, is to immediately channel the results in a *permanent form* of witnessing. If you try, instead, to follow immediately with mass evangelism, you are actually preventing your church from going into a permanent form of evangelism.

There is a long look to be taken in evangelism, though an evangelist, eager for immediate results, may not see this at first. We need to begin thinking in terms of long range results.

A campaign in mass evangelism that comes right after a great effort in witnessing, always focuses the attention on the evangelist. The people fail to see their own great contribution. They fail to see that this kind of results could come *every week* as a natural part of the church's life. The layman never gets the full impact of knowing how powerful personal evangelism is. This knowledge is essential. Instead, unconsciously, the credit for all the results is shifted to the evangelist.

Personal evangelism gets *interrupted* at the most critical point — the point of sustaining results. The interruption can never quite be bridged.

Personal evangelism has always played the part of "helper" to something else. If ever personal evangelism is to be reclaimed it *must be elevated to the same level* as mass evangelism. Mass evangelism has held sway for several hundreds of years. It can step down for a season to make possible the rebirth of personal evangelism.

Also, a revival meeting (evangelistic campaign) is always followed by a period of complete physical exhaustion. Such physical exhaustion automatically rules out any hopes of shifting immediately into a strong program of weekly visitation.

The very opposite is true at the end of a two-week campaign in witnessing. You can actually expect the weekly visitation program to grow!

Separate the two — campaigns in mass and in personal evangelism. Concentrate on a great thrust in personal witnessing, and your people can get the full impact of what their own witness can do.

Personal evangelism, once it is truly set in motion, can sustain itself. Don't let it stumble, in its infancy, on traditionally set patterns.

WHEN PERSONAL AND MASS EVANGELISM
CAN BE COMBINED

When can these two kinds of campaigns be combined? The answer is simple: when there is something to combine!*

When your church has a strong nucleus of well-trained, consistent, and high caliber soul winners, then you can think in terms of combining the two.

You should not attempt to wed the two until your church has gone through *at least two* successful campaigns in personal evangelism, *and* until your new weekly visitation program is at least a year old.

We might add one other observation that has already been noted. A well-planned, well executed (and well prayed for) Campaign in Personal Witnessing will always bring in *at least as* great a harvest of souls as will any venture in mass evangelism.

The next six chapters explain in detail how to have a Campaign in Personal Evangelism. This Campaign builds a foundation upon which you can grow a soul winning church. The remainder of the book explains how you can sustain the results of the Campaign, and how to have a perennial harvest of souls.

---

*Certainly a pastor should put emphasis on soul winning during a mass evangelism campaign. The point here is the need of keeping a personal evangelism *campaign* separated from a mass evangelism *campaign,* until personal evangelism in your church is full grown.

CHAPTER 16

THE PASTOR TAKES STEP ONE

"I have tried everything, but my people just will not win souls. My church is different."

Here is an often made statement by many pastors.

What is the reason for such fruitless results, after so noble an effort to grow a soul winning church?

In most cases, such failure follows a definite pattern.

The pastor sees the need of soul winning in his own life, and in the life of his people. His burden becomes acute. In his desire to become a soul winner himself, he launches his church into a great evangelistic venture. From it, he hopes to become an effective soul winner, and *at the same time*, bring his people into a similar experience.

This is just impossible.

The greatest error a pastor can make, as he plans to lead his people into the experience of soul winning, is to assume that both he and his people can have this new experience *at the same time*.

As hard a pill as this is to swallow, and as lonely an experience as it is, the pastor must "go it alone" in the beginning. Later, he can lead his people into the same adventure. But it must happen to him *first*. After that, the experience must mature in his life before he can ever hope to share it with his people.

Throughout this book, there is a constant theme, that you do not create an evangelistic church by a series of new methods, as much as you do by a spiritual experience with God. That spiritual upheaval must begin in the life of the pastor.

FIRST:

Immerse yourself in the soul winning concept as presented in this book.

Master the concept. Know it by heart. Become a scientist in it!

At the very same time, — and even more important — seek God! If you do not thoroughly understand the Spirit Filled Life — and for most of us this is also a new discovery — then let God's Word teach it to you. Claim this life, by faith, as *your* life.

Then, and then only, go out and start winning men to Christ in your community! Don't stop until you have won *one*. Don't stop then either! Keep going out and winning men to Christ *until these new converts start filling up empty spaces* in your church pews.

Concentrate on your personal need of winning souls, and the need of the Holy Spirit operating in your life.

Let your people *see*, not hear, what has happened to you. They must *see* some of the people you are winning! Let them see your concern, yes; but also your *victory!*

Then, and then only, are you ready to begin preaching about soul winning. Then, and then only, are you ready to begin drawing up plans and launching a program to have a soul winning church. Then, and then only, will your people follow you!

And will they follow you? Oh, my brother, will they ever! They will follow you through hell and fire and smoke and glory! Why? Because *you* have earned the right to be heard and followed. They will follow you. If you should think not, try and see!

There is a lot of mythical thinking at this point. To illustrate:

A pastor asked the author to personally tutor him in soul winning methods and in the mechanics of visitation. When this first point was made ("You must earn the right to be followed"), he countered, "Why, I win souls all the time." When this point came up again, he exclaimed, "Look, I can't spend all my time winning souls." (Which is true. There is no one area of the Christian life to go to seed on. And right now there are a dozen areas of

Christian endeavor in as poor a state of repair as is personal evangelism.)

One evening, a few days later, this pastor won a man to Christ while out visiting. He started telling everyone, overjoyed. No one could have predicted the results. Word spread to the whole church family. The author heard the story recounted many times from the people. They were overjoyed at this great event.

This was the same pastor who had said, "I win souls all the time".

(You might think they would have said to him, "Well, you're a preacher; what are you so excited about? You should have been doing this for years." But laymen never think this way about it. They are always thrilled at the news that their pastor is winning souls.)

Here is the point: don't try to get your people to win souls until *after* you are winning a host of people yourself. Don't even think about a soul winning church until *you, yourself,* have brought a host of new converts into the church . . . on your own!

After you have had a consistent witness in your own life for several months, and the "sheaves have been brought in", then there are some other problems to face up to, and some life-changing resolutions to make.

Set some goals.

It has already been pointed out that there must come a radical change in the church's activities, and in the attitude toward conformity. Finally, you must come to grips with the true purpose of the church in evangelism.

The purpose of *your* church is to evangelize your community. Set a goal in your heart that together you will evangelize the entire world . . . the world of your community! Determine that you and your people will knock on every door and witness in every living room until you can say you have totally evangelized your community . . . until you can say: "Our church has matched the work of the First century church in Jerusalem!"

Do you realize that if every evangelistically minded pastor in America would set this very simple goal, and then lead his people out to witness in *every* home, that we could probably *totally evangelize North America in* one or two years? Think of it! How easy it would be for every church to witness in every home in its community. Undoubtedly, this event would be accompanied by the greatest revival and turning to God in *world history!*

Draw a circle around your life, and regardless of what others *ever* do, resolve to be obedient in the area over which *you* are responsible.

CHAPTER 17

STEP TWO

HOW TO TAKE A RELIGIOUS CENSUS

After the pastor has prepared himself, he must begin preparing his church. The first step — chronologically — is to locate prospects.

In Part II of this book you read of the need of a new approach to this problem. Here is a simple plan for taking a religious census that can be 100 per cent accurate. When it is finished it will be 100 per cent complete, having reached every human being in your community.

WHEN TO TAKE THE CENSUS

Preparation for the census should begin at least one month *before* the census. The census should be over and out of the way at least two months before the Soul Winning Campaign begins. So census preparation should begin at least *three months* before the Campaign does.

STEP I—Decide on the area to be surveyed.

Get a large map of your community. Study it closely. Decide on the exact territory you are going to survey. The area you mark off becomes your "world". This is your *Jerusalem!*

(1) If your "world" is too large for the size of your church at the present time, begin with a small area.

(2) If you plan to move your church building soon, you may desire to survey the new area.

(3) Let the area you survey fall into very natural geographical boundaries.

(4) If you are surrounded by near-by churches of your own denomination, feel free to survey the area around them. NO sheep stealing though. Stick to evangelistic prospects when visiting those areas later on.

STEP II—List every street in the area you have marked off.

Make a list of every street that is in the area you have marked off. Now take blank sheets of paper and have one street name listed at the top of each sheet.

You are then ready for:

STEP III—The Street Canvass.

The next step is a Street Canvass. The purpose of the street canvass is to locate the correct address of every house in your community. There is only one way to make sure that *every* house in the community is covered. That is by getting the house numbers off the houses! Experience has proven all other methods inadequate.

The pastor should engage one of the women's organizations of the church to do this job.

Here's how to take a street canvass:

(1) Assign a street to two ladies. One will drive the car, while the other will write down house numbers.

(2) The ladies will drive down the street slowly, while one lady writes down the house numbers of every house onto the paper.

(3) If a home has no number, it can usually be determined by comparing the house number on the two houses on each side. If this proves inadequate, stop the car, go to the home, explain the purpose of the call, and ask the residents what their correct address is.

Continue the street canvass until you have the correct house number of every house, apartment house, trailer court, etc. on *every* street in your community.

STEP IV—Transfer the street canvass information onto the census cards.

Now take the results of the street canvass, and have these results copied *in ink*, or *typed*, onto the blank census cards. When you finish this job, there should be a blank census card with an address typed on it. There should be one card for every address in your community.

NOTE:

(1) Apartment houses should have *one card* for every *apartment*, with the apartment number also listed on it; a trailer court should have a card for every house trailer.

(2) Don't attempt to substitute a city directory or criss-cross telephone directory for a street canvass. Both are inadequate for 100 per cent coverage and 100 per cent accuracy.

(3) By having a card for every house, later when you take the census you will know exactly which houses have been missed during the census. You can continue taking the census until all the cards are filled in. You will know exactly when the religious census is complete. There will be no blank cards left!

(4) When you have completed transferring the addresses onto the cards, place all the cards in a box and arrange the cards in the file box *by streets*. You should have a "street divider" card to divide each street. (This is an indexed card with the street's name written on the index tab.) This index card keeps the streets separated.*

PREPARATION FOR THE RELIGIOUS CENSUS

To have a really effective census, with a large turnout of workers, you need to do a good job of publicizing the religious census. Publicity should begin one month before Census Day.

---

*It is usually best to arrange the streets in the box by alphabetizing the names of the streets.

How To Set a Date:

Sunday afternoon is almost always the best day for a census. A week day might find a few more people at home, but you will not have a good turn-out of workers.

The date of the census should be set at least two months before the Campaign in Personal Evangelism.

It should also be set far enough ahead to give you an opportunity to get all your materials together.

Plan a Meal

When Christians spend all Sunday afternoon out taking a census, they automatically miss the opportunity to prepare one of their meals at home. So plan to serve a meal at the church. If you begin the census early (1:30 p.m.) then have a meal right after the Sunday morning service. If you begin after 3:00 p.m. serve the evening meal after the census is over. (The *noon* meal will produce more workers.)

How to Publicize

Use every normal channel of church publicity:

(1) The church bulletin and the paper.
(2) Prepare a bulletin insert.
(3) Have someone prepare large posters to place up throughout the building.
(4) Use the announcement period in the church service.
(5) Announcements in Sunday School classes.

You will also want to prepare a *commitment card*. This card should be passed out to everyone, and they should be asked to sign it. (The best appeal may be: "It is necessary that we know as soon as possible how many will work in the census so that we can know how many to expect for the meal. Please sign the card now.") Pass this card out on the *two* Sundays preceding the Sunday of the census.

Make an announcement in the local newspaper. This will alert the residents to expect church callers.

Also, many churches give each census taker a hat—a small white hat made of paper, like a butcher's hat—and a badge with their name on it. For some reason, this "official" look gives the workers courage, and produces a very cooperative response from those who are interviewed. You might consider using these.

Each census taker will need a ball point *pen*. You might consider giving that as a gift to each worker. A *clipboard* might be used by each worker.

Make your decision about each of these items. Plan to have all of them on hand well ahead of Census Day.

TRAINING THE CENSUS TAKERS

Here's how to train your workers on Census Day, so their cards will be accurate and legible.

Make the Census Day meal as delightful as possible. An atmosphere of excitement needs to be created throughout this entire venture. After the meal is over, gather the group together for training:

(1) Give each person ONE *blank* card.
(2) Pass out the paper hats, lapel pins, clip boards. Make sure everyone has a ball point pen.

Now Give A Demonstration

Have someone to stand with you in front of the group. (Practice this demonstration together beforehand.) Let him play the part of the home owner. You be the census taker. Tell the group to follow each question carefully. Tell them to keep an eye on their own blank card, and watch each step you take.

After this demonstration is over, ask for questions.

(Here's a hint: Tell the worker to look *down at the card* when asking people about their ages. This totally eliminates embarrassment.)

Now Repeat The Demonstration

Go through the entire demonstration a *second*

time. Only this time, have each person in the room fill in the answers right along with you. When this is over, have every person pass in his cards for "grading". This need only take a moment, and serves mostly to get each person to do his best.

Lastly, tell everyone to re-check his cards after he has gone to three or four houses. The worker can inspect his own work to see if he is filling in all the information and writing plainly.

HOW TO GIVE THE DEMONSTRATION

At the Door, the surveyor says:

"Good afternoon, I'm Bill Jones. I am from the _____ Church. We are taking a religious survey this afternoon. Perhaps you have noticed the announcement in the papers that workers would be calling and asking a few questions? I don't need to come in, but would appreciate it if you could take a minute to help us."

Hint: Have your audience repeat these words aloud, following you in unison.

Explain The Census Cards To The Workers.

Give careful attention to each point on the card, reminding the workers there are (ten) questions. Naturally, they are to be warm and friendly, but the survey time ought not to be prolonged by dealing with other things. Getting the card filled out is the object.

As you explain the card, your people will begin to see the significance of the ten questions. There are no lines to memorize, other than the opener. After that the census taker need only read the questions from the card and write down the responses. A householder will usually agree to the request, to which the worker can respond a cheery, "Okay, then, here we go."

QUESTION 1. "What is your last name?"

Space for the answer is found at top-center of the card. Enter the last name of the family living there. Also, note, if it is a trailer park or motel. Some trailer courts have permanent guests.

2. What is your telephone number?"

This question is easily missed. Also, be sure to get the exchange or prefix to the number.

3. "What is Your name?"

After you get the name of the person you are talking to, secure the names of every person in the family. There could be different names, as sometimes occurs in remarriage.

4. "What is your birthday?" (Or, "year of birth")

Some churches prefer, "What is the date of your birth?"

Note: Tell your people that very few individuals mind giving their ages. Surveys show this. The reluctance is usually with the census taker, not the householder.

Some census takers find it hard to ask this question, no matter how well they have been trained. They seem to "freeze" at this point, and can't get the question out. Because of this, the card should contain an "Age Estimator". The census taker can check the age bracket as he walks away from the interview. Some indication must go on the card, and while the estimator is not the best way, it is better than no information at all.

5. "Are you a member of a church?"

Census takers often use a check mark to

answer this question. But a check can mean either yes or no. The card has space for the correct answer, and the census taker should be instructed to use it.

6-8. "If so, what denomination?"

These questions are designed to gain information about church members. It is not enough to know, for example, that they are Baptists and members of First Baptist Church. The *town* in which their church is located is important. People have been mistakenly marked off as *Not Prospects* because it was assumed their church was in the town where they lived, while in reality, they belonged to a church in another city.

9-10. "Are you active in Sunday School and church?" (check.)

"How often do you attend?"

These questions serve a two-fold purpose. They show whether the people are actually enrolled in a Sunday School. If they are church members, but NOT enrolled in a Sunday School, it indicates they are probably INACTIVE church members, and possibly eligible for visitation.

Instruct the workers to watch the *way* the person at the door answers "How often do you attend church?" The way he answers is as important as the words he says. You can tell if a person is actually attending regularly by the way he answers, plus what he says.

Remember, these questions must be asked about *every* member of the family, *not* just the person you are talking to.

Now turn the card over, and call attention to an item on the back.

There are (six) places for entering information, but the one on the upper left is for the *census* taker. He enters his name and any comment or word about the family. (Sickness could be a possible entry.) If the worker should use this space, then he enters his name in the place marked "surveyed by", and notes his comments in the space. The other spaces on the back are for future visits, and have no meaning for the census taker.

If no one is at home, the card is left blank. No entry is made at all. The fact the card remains blank indicates no interview has been made, and that a return trip will be necessary.

GIVING OUT CARDS

Give each worker about 40 cards. Do not send them out in pairs. You may, though, decide to send two people out to work *one street*. It is encouraging to be able to look across the street and see a Christian friend doing what you are doing, and realize that you are not alone.

Have prayer, and dismiss the group. The census has begun!

HOW TO COMPLETE THE CENSUS

When the workers return, you may be amazed to find only about 50 per cent of the cards filled in. Fortunately, though, you can tell *exactly which* homes were not contacted. The blank cards with house numbers on them tell you this. (This is where the "street canvass" begins to be very valuable.)

You are now faced with the problem of *how* to *finish* this census.

It is not wise to try to have another Census Day. Good response for a Census Day is a "one shot" item.

Here are three alternatives:

1. Hire a group of ladies to finish the job. This is by far the best way. In this way, they can return again and again to homes that were missed before. And also, you can demand a degree of quality.

2. Get a volunteer group of ladies to finish the census.

3. Get a criss-cross telephone directory to call as many as possible. (About 25 per cent of the people in your community will not be listed in this directory.) Finish the remaining cards with paid or volunteer workers.

DON'T STOP UNTIL YOU HAVE SURVEYED *EVERY* HOME.

HOW TO DECIDE WHAT A PROSPECT IS

What is an evangelistic prospect? This is one major problem which this book seeks to solve.

When most churches finish a census, they will flip through the cards and take out all the cards of people who are "unchurched". Then they remove all the cards of inactive members of their denomination . . . And throw all the other cards away!!

When a pastor throws these "left over" cards away (usually 80 per cent of the census cards) he actually throws away most of his *evangelistic prospects!*

Why?

We must face a hard, but true, fact: most people in America *are* church members; yet, most people *never* attend church. Too, *many* prospects say they are church members, who are not; Many were brought into the church as infants or very small children, and have rarely been back to church since. These people are as "unchurched" as any people on earth. They have only a denominational inheritance.

Here is a very hard but important fact: a large segment of present-day churches no longer present the need of conversion. Many churches have not preached "experiential salvation" for nearly a century.

A large segment of American church members are UNSAVED.

A PLAN

Here is the purpose of your religious census:

NOT just to locate those who profess no church membership

NOT just to locate your own denominational prospects

BUT:

TO LOCATE EVERYONE IN YOUR ENTIRE COMMUNITY WHO NEVER ATTENDS CHURCH . . . Regardless of denomination.

Christians from your church will visit ALL these people (during the Campaign and in the regular weekly visitation program that follows.)

The Christians do not go to these homes assuming the people are lost. Nor do they assume that they are truly converted. The Christian goes to every home to DISCOVER! . . . To discover whether the person is saved *or* lost!

(In another part of this book, there is a section which discusses exactly how Christians can go to the home of *all* the inactive church members in your community and find out if they are truly born again. Christians can find this out without asking a direct question. The unconverted will tell them, without even knowing it.)

(See chapter entitled "A New Concept in Soul Winning Methods".)

In summing up: most of the people in your community say they belong to a church. Most of the people in your community never attend church. A large number of these church members are unsaved. There is a way for Christians from your church to visit all these people and find out if they are lost or saved. This can be done without actually asking a direct question.

You will want to plan to send your people to every home in the community where the family never attends church. Your people may discover they are lost. If so, they can seek to win them, and they can also record the discovery on the back of the prospect card for future visits.

Inactive church members make up the largest segment of your prospects. These people are the great "unknown quantity" of every community. They need Christ, and their hearts are even hungrier for Him, though they themselves do not realize it. And they can be won!! By treating these as potential prospects, you can actually guadruple the number of prospects that a church usually has.

TABULATING THE RESULTS OF THE CENSUS

After the census is over, tabulate the results. This will be easy if you use the Census Card illustrated on Page 248. Use one tab for each person. Place each tab on the *scale* printed at the top of the card; put the tab in the place that corresponds with the information on the card.

There are three types of prospects.

1. DENOMINATIONAL—people who are members of your denomination, but who are INACTIVE.

2. EVANGELISTIC—those acknowledging they are not Christians.

3. THE DOUBTFUL—those who may profess some kind of church membership, but who never attend church, and whose attitude indicates they need spiritual help. (These are the ones to visit for the purpose of *discovering* their true relationship to Christ.)

DO NOT THROW AWAY THE REST OF THE CARDS

What can you do with the rest of the cards? These are cards of people who are *active* church members of some church in the community. They certainly are not prospects for your church. Keep them!

They may not be prospects, true. They may all be very active members of other churches. Remember this, though. The cards represent not only people, but also *houses*. People move. Houses do not.

In the next twelve months, *one* out of every *five* families in that stack of cards will move out! Someone else will move into the vacant house to take their place. These NEW people may turn out to be prospects. So keep the cards. They give you a record of houses. It is just as important to know who are *not* prospects, as it is to know who are.

If you, or the church secretary, will compare the Newcomers List to your prospect file, you can keep up with all the new, potential prospects who move in. By doing this, you automatically keep the entire file up to date.*

(If you use the card concept illustrated in this book, you can drop all the "not prospect" cards right into the prospect box with the rest of the cards. Just don't put any tabs on them, and they will not get in the way. They will be available when you need them. If you don't want to put them in the same box, keep them separated, but keep them handy, so that they can be checked each week against the Newcomers List.)

INSTRUCTIONS TO DOWNTOWN CHURCHES

The downtown church has many problems and difficulties that other churches do not face. Because there is no residential community in the downtown area, these

---

* See "The Visitation Program". How to keep the prospect cards up to date. (Chapter 23)

churches often find it hard to take a religious census. Here are some suggestions.

1. Keep a constant internal census going. Downtown churches usually have many Sunday visitors (more than other churches) and you can concentrate on reaching them in your visitation program.

2. Find a residential area in your city where there is no church of your denomination and concentrate your efforts of visiting in that area.

3. Find out which area of the city most of your members come from, and carry on a survey of that area. Church members may not be prospects for your church in these areas, but you should consider *lost* people as prospects regardless of what part of town you discover them.

4. Here is a little known and terribly overlooked fact. The average downtown area of a city contains at least *five* per cent of the city's population! Even the downtown church has a residential area right under its own shadow. Large numbers of people live in downtown apartment houses, hotels, motels, and even in office buildings. Do not overlook the possibility of taking a religious census in the downtown area. Also, don't forget the slum houses and hotels where your church can have a dynamic ministry.

5. Depend strongly on your newcomers list. The great soul winning churches in America that are down town find their best source of growth to be this: *be the first ones to the homes of newcomers.* The church gives help to the family lacking spiritual growth, and wins the lost. The downtown church can grow this way!

The downtown church should never forget that people who are *lost* are prospects for the downtown church, no matter where they live. You cannot always go into suburban areas to do denominational visitation, but the field is

171

the world among the *lost*. The church may be hesitant to encourage people to move their membership to the downtown church when they live next door to a suburban church. This is not true when the people are unsaved. The downtown church, more than any other, should be one of soul winners and of evangelism. There are no limits to the prospects when the downtown church dedicates itself to this task.

INSTRUCTIONS TO RURAL CHURCHES

The rural church is also faced with a peculiar set of problems when taking a religious census. Usually the streets and roads around the rural church are not named. Very rarely will the houses in the rural areas have house numbers.

Here's what to do:

1. Get a map of your county (from the county court house).
2. Locate the rural area around your church on the map.
3. Get a large board, blow up the map of the community by retracing it to a larger scale on the board.
4. Place a thumb tack in every place where there is a house. Continue doing this until you have one thumb tack on the map for every house in the community.
5. Give names to the roads and number the houses (thumb tacks) on your map.
6. Do the same thing with your census cards. Put the name of the road on the card, as well as the corresponding number that you have given the house.

Now you will find it very easy to send your people out into the community to take the religious census. You will also find it easy to make visitation assignments each week. The workers will need only to refer to the large map you have made in order to locate the houses they are going to visit.

THE SIMPLEST RELIGIOUS CENSUS IN THE WORLD:

One last word. Here is a suggestion for the simplest religious census possible.

First, take a street canvass. Have a card made out for every house in your entire community. Then, instead of taking a religious census, launch a visitation program. One night a week, your people can begin calling on the homes in your community. When they go into the home, they can sit there for a pleasant visit. While there, they can ask permission for some "religious information" just before they go.

Continue this until your people have paid a visit to *every* home in your community. This is a terrific way to really get to know the community and all the people in it, and discover the real spiritual condition of everyone.

The one drawback: it may take as long as a year! (If your people can witness on each visit, as well as take down the information, then there are no drawbacks. This procedure works very well when you begin it right after a Campaign In Personal Evangelism. You can know you have totally evangelized your community when the census is over!!)

After you have finished your census, and set up a prospect file system, you are ready to start laying plans for a Campaign in Personal Evangelism.

CHAPTER 18

STEP THREE

PLAN THE CAMPAIGN

A Campaign in Personal Evangelism calls for as much intensive planning and preparation as any venture in mass evangelism that your church has ever undertaken.

Following is a very workable plan for your Campaign.

Keep in mind what the purpose of a Campaign in Soul Winning is:

1. To win souls—just like any undertaking in evangelism
2. To train your people in soul winning, and make them soul winners.
3. To lay a foundation upon which you can build a permanent, perennial program of evangelism.
4. To introduce and discipline your people to a new routine in visitation and evangelism.

Preliminary Decisions:

Set a *date* for the Campaign. The date should be set a minimum of *three* months before the Campaign actually begins. Even this is rather brief. If the Campaign is set *that* soon, then begin preparation *immediately*.

Make arrangements for *finances*. One of the nice things about Personal Evangelism is that these Campaigns are inexpensive. No publicity is needed outside the church building. Expensive outside publicity such as mass evangelism depends on, is *un*necessary. Still, a great deal of promotion will be needed *within* the church, and a budget needs to be set up.

Draw Up A Schedule

When you have finished reading the next two chapters, draw up a "Schedule of Preparation". Sit down with a calendar and write in dates for each step of preparation. Put down the date to start each step, and the date it is to be finished. Write down the exact date each piece of publicity is to appear.

Draw Up A "Year's Calendar Of Evangelism"

When you have finished this book, draw up a "Year's Calendar Of Evangelism". (Study the chapter on "Sustained Evangelism" for drawing up your calendar.) You must have a *planned* program to sustain soul winning for the first year. After the first year, Soul Winning will prove to be relatively easy to sustain, for it will be so much a part of the church's life, and the people will have a consuming desire to continue winning others to Christ.

Meet With Your Church Leaders

Get with your key leaders, either informally at a meal, or in a called meeting. Present the concept you are about to launch into. Explain the purpose of the Campaign in Personal Evangelism. Show them what must be done.

Sell them on the idea. Get their wholehearted support.

Cut Down On Activities:

Launching a program which is ultimately designed to evangelize an entire town, takes some doing. For at least two months, all your attention should be focused on getting this undertaking into action. Focusing this much attention on soul winning will, in itself, be a new experience for everyone. The people will grasp the importance of the coming campaign because of the thorough preparation, and the dedication you are asking of them.

(Remember, too, that you must personally precede all this with several months of intense soul winning. You must make a great stride forward in your own life of witnessing, and bringing new converts into the church.)

Go over the entire plan with your church staff (should your church be large enough to have a staff). Drill them in this new concept of an evangelistic campaign until they are as articulate in it as you are. Also, begin with your staff to make an appeal toward a spiritual deepening of their lives.

Listed below are the different areas of activity that call for thorough preparation. Be very wise in selecting Christians to carry out this work; and check them constantly for progress. Keep them to a *time schedule*.

1.

COMPILE INFORMATION ON
THE COMMUNITY'S SPIRITUAL CONDITION
(Community Research)

In the weeks of preparation ahead, there will be a great deal of need for statistical data for messages, for promotional material, etc. Set someone to the task of compiling this information. Here are a few things that need to be discovered, and then reported:

The population of the immediate community

How many churches in that area

The total membership of each church

The total membership of all churches combined

The average attendance in each church

The combined total attendance of all churches

Age breakdown of new converts in your church and how they were won.

A five-year study of past evangelistic results in your church

Your church's net growth in the last five years.

Find out from some county official, or your Chamber of Commerce, the number of people moving into your town, its *rate of growth* or decline.

A study should also be made of your *denomination's evangelistic accomplishments*. This information is probably available from some department within the denomination.

Add to this list usable statistics in this book, and information from other sources which have bearing on your Campaign.

Make a thorough *study* of the *religious census* you have taken. These results need to be published widely throughout the church.

Compile all the above information together. It should be made available to those working in other areas of preparation for the Campaign, so that they can incorporate it into the material they are preparing.

2.

PUBLICITY PREPARATION

Those charged with preparing the publicity for this campaign have one of the most weighty responsibilities. Keep in mind that a Campaign in Personal Evangelism is a *new* idea. It will need an *extra* amount of publicity. The people will have to be educated to the concept. This means repeating a few facts over and over.

When those preparing the publicity meet together, their first step might be to *read this chapter*, and then . . .

Draw Up A Publicity Calendar

Decide on exactly what publicity will be prepared. Sit down with a calendar. Write in the exact date this material has to be put to use. Then back up several weeks and write in the day to begin preparing it.

Stick to Schedule. Get the material into service on the date set.

Coordinate Your Publicity

There will be several other groups working on other projects. They may need publicity help for their projects. Coordinate the needs and the use of the publicity.

A Campaign Paper

The backbone of the campaign is the "Campaign Paper". This should be mailed out once a week for *four* weeks, to every family in the church.

The paper should be educational and informative, as to personal evangelism in general, and the Campaign in particular. The pastor should decide what goes into the paper. Someone must be in charge of correlating the articles and getting the paper out on time.

Print or mimeograph the campaign paper, as finances permit. Use pictures wherever possible.

Bulletin Inserts:

At least two bulletin inserts should be prepared to go into the Sunday bulletins. One should be used *two weeks* before the Campaign, the other *one* week before. One should be educational, explaining what the campaign is. The other should have the schedule of events for the two weeks, along with illustrative material. (Use *both* sides of the Bulletin Inserts —an illustration on one side, and information on the other.)

Publicity In Every Class Room

There should be a poster or "streamer" in *every* class room in the church building. A simple theme should be carried out, such as "A Week of Training —A Week of Visiting"; or "Back the Campaign in Personal Evangelism"; or "One Solid Week of Visiting".

If possible, the date of the Campaign should be on this poster.

These should go up *four* weeks before the Campaign begins. Place the poster up just behind where the teacher stands, so that all eyes will see it.

A Large (Auditorium Size) Banner

A large banner (approximately 4' x 25') might be stretched across some conspicuous place. It might read, "Let's Win the World, Of Our Community". There might be interposed a drawing of your town with a picture of the world.

This Banner should be up *three* Sundays before the Campaign.

Large Posters

Several (2 to 4) large posters (approximately 4' x 6') should be placed up conspicuously in the church buildings. The theme can be simple: "Our Church in Soul Winning Training", or "You Can Be a Soul Winner", etc. Add the dates of the Campaign.

Place these posters up three Sundays before the Campaign.

Large Chart

After consulting with those in charge of "community research", and studying the figures compiled on the religious census, some very interesting facts may be available. These facts, or statistics, could be listed on a large chart or graft (approximately 4' wide and 8' tall) and hung in some obvious place for study and discussion.

The Campaign Paper, which has already been mentioned, is a major key to success. It needs to contain dates and places of *all* meetings. It should serve as a challenge to prayer, as well as listing places of prayer meetings, etc. Facts about great soul winners, or soul winning churches, should be included, as should be a scriptural study of the New Testament pattern of evangelism. This paper serves to coordinate and publicize all of the Campaign.

There are several facts that must be emphasized over

and over. One is that this is a *two week* meeting. Another is that there is one *whole* week given over to visiting. Repeat the New Testament theme. Emphasize one or two Scriptures over and over.

Your church should become informed and then convinced *that its job is to evangelize the entire community*.

COMMITMENT COMMITTEE

The pastor should select a group of men and women to serve as a "Speakers Bureau" or "Commitment Committee".

Here is their job:

One person should attend every church-related meeting and function that meets during the month preceding the campaign. He should attend in an "official" capacity. His job is to bring a very brief word about the Campaign, and a word to encourage everyone to participate. For one month, some Christian should visit every class party, every organizational or departmental meeting of the church. Some of the "spot announcements" that he makes should be in the way of a personal testimony about witnessing, then a word about the coming Campaign and what it can mean to the entire church.

In the *last* two weeks of preparation, someone should go into every Sunday School class and take about 30 seconds to remind everyone to participate in the Campaign.

(You may decide to use commitment cards. If so, give these cards to each person serving on the "Commitment Committee", and let them pass the cards out in every meeting they attend, and take up the cards after they have been signed.)

Assign each worker certain activities or meetings to attend. Explain exactly what is to be said to each group.

PREPARE A VISITATION PACKET

There are certain tools that are to be used during the Week of Visiting. These tools will continue to be used in the regular visitation program that follows after the Campaign ends. One of these is the *Visitation Packet.*

These packets need to be finished *before* the Campaign begins, for the packet will be introduced during the Week of Training. It will take several weeks to compile the materials that go in the packet, so begin early.

A visitation packet is used by each couple that goes visiting.

How to make the Visitation Packet:*

Have some two-ply index paper cut into 10"x10" sheets. Fold up three inches of the bottom. Then staple the top corners of the three inch edges. Fold the index paper down the middle (vertically), and you have a folder with 2 pockets, in which to insert materials.

Here is what should go into the Packet:

(More will be said about its use in the chapter on the Week of Visiting.)

1. Church Publicity:

Your church probably has a nice piece of church publicity, or an information folder, about the church. If not, have some prepared. Several of these folders should go into each packet. If your church cannot afford publicity (!) then use your church's bulletin.

2. Evangelistic Tracts.

Carefully select two or three *well written* evangelistic tracts (in color if possible, with content—not just Scriptures). Several of these should go into each packet.

3. Helps For New Converts

There are very few booklets in print, small enough to go into a Visitation Packet, which have

___
* See the chapter entitled "The Visitation Program" explaining how to use this packet. Chapter 23)

been specifically designed to give to a new convert in the moment after conversion. For this reason, *The First Epistle of St. John* is recommended. Check the bibliography for sources.

Place several in each packet.

4. A Map of the Community

Try to find a map that is small enough to fit into the visitation packet. Place a copy of this map in each packet. (Reduce the map to size if necessary.) If you have a rural community, either hang a large map up in the church building, or mimeograph a community map.

5. Census Card

Every packet should have some blank census cards in it.

Order New Testaments

Every Christian will need to carry a New Testament during the Week of Visiting. A large number of Christians will want one. The church should also keep some on hand at all times.

Order New Testaments well in advance of the meeting.

Also Purchase:

From 50 to 100 U. S. Postal Cards, and have them rubber stamped with the church's address on the front of the cards. These will be needed in the visitation program.

Also order a large number of extra evangelistic tracts. These will be passed out by Christians during the Week of Visiting.

Preparing From The Pulpit

The pastor will be faced with the need of emphasizing

the message of personal evangelism from the pulpit. Here are some graphic passages that deal with the subject:

Luke 14:16-23   A modern day explanation of "streets". What the "streets, lanes, city, highways, hedges" are for us today.

Matt. 25:31-46   A dramatic presentation of the need of personal Christianity.

Luke 10:1-12   The first visitation program, and
(Matt. 10:1-42)   its results.

The Book of Acts   A study of the early church's program of personal evangelism.

Also! The pastor has already been advised to give special attention to his own life, and the Holy Spirit. This is a vital relationship necessary to anyone who would win souls. Moreover, it is a relation that is essential to successfully living the Christian life.

This is an experience you must pass on to your people. They, too, must be called upon to obey the Scriptural command to "be filled with the Holy Spirit"! It is up to the pastor to show his people *how* to be filled with the Spirit, and how to *walk* in the Spirit.

CHAPTER 19

MAKE A SURVEY OF
NEGLECTED COMMUNITY OPPORTUNITIES.

Have you ever thought of invading the "honky tonks" and beer taverns in your community for Christ?

Did you ever think about the hotels in your community as a place to do regular visitation?

If not, you are overlooking some of the best, and most exciting, opportunities of witnessing for Christ.

There are many overlooked opportunities of evangelism around every church. One phase of preparing for a Campaign in Personal Evangelism is discovering the "unevangelized" areas in the world around your church. Going out to discover this neglected area of your town can be enthralling. If possible, the pastor should help in this task. Before anyone else, he needs to be familiar with the "unevangelized areas" in the community. The success of the Week of Visiting is very dependent on the information you gather.

This chapter will give you an idea of where to look. Keep a record of your findings. You will need all this information in planning the Week of Visiting.

Make A List Of The Hotels And Motels In The Community.

List the names and addresses of all the hotels and motels in your area. List every hotel, no matter how luxurious or how poor. Call the manager, explain who you are, and ask if there are any people who have *permanent residence* in the hotel. You may be amazed to find there always are some, and often many! The same is true of "boarding houses".

This is perhaps the most overlooked source of prospects there is. Make plans to have laymen from your church visit these people during the Week of Visiting.

Make A List Of All Hospitals In Your Community.

This should also include all the following:

> Rest homes
> Old Folks Homes
> Sanitoriums
> Institutes for the blind, deaf, handicapped, etc.

How To Use This Information:

List the name and address of the institution. Find out exactly who is in charge. You will want to make plans to send a group of Christians to each one of these places during the Week of Visitation.

Decide on about how many Christians will be needed to go to each place. (Visiting in hospitals is an area in which ladies serve best.) Decide on a tentative schedule. Then contact the person in charge of the institution. Explain that you are having an emphasis on visitation in your church. Explain that you want some of your members to pay a visit there (to visit those who can receive visitors). In some of these institutions, you will be given permission to put on a simple religious program. In a hospital, it will be a matter of visiting "bed to bed".

Ask for permission to visit the institution. Set a date and a time. Place this information on your Campaign schedule.

Make A List Of All Government Projects:

Military bases	Labor Camps
Army, Navy,	Special Housing Projects
Air Force, etc.	

Make A List Of All Institutions Of Learning:

Colleges	Technical Schools
Nursing Schools	Orphanages, etc.

How to Use This Information:

In most every community, there is a nearby college, military base, or the like. Most are grossly neglected spiritually. You should consider setting up a permanent ministry for each one. You might even study the program of inter-denominational organizations that have been formed especially to give emphasis to these groups. You will find some helpful ideas that will guide you in creating a program for your church.

You will need special permission to send visitors to some of these places, such as military bases. In other areas, such as boys dormitories, young men from your church can go without making previous arrangements.

A real ministry awaits a church at colleges, in the dormitories, at the campuses, and wherever there are large groups of young people living together.

NOTE:

In making arrangements to visit these institutions, cast about in your mind for someone in your church who can help you in gaining the permission you need. (eg., a doctor in your church might help make arrangements in the hospitals; a service man, the military base; a policeman, the jail; etc.)

Make A List Of Penal Institutions.

Jail	Reformatory
Penitentiary	Labor Farm

(Also benevolent institutions, such as homes for unwed mothers, alcoholic recovery institutions, etc.)

Here again, are institutions where your church can—and should—start a program of evangelism. Get acquainted with those who manage these places.

Schedule a time, during the Week of Visiting, when Christians from your church can go there—to do personal work, or to present a program in music and Word.

Do not overlook women in penitentiaries and jails. Here is a real place of witness for Christian ladies.

Visiting these institutions can be one of the most fruitful and soul gripping events of the Week of Visiting.

Be sure to print, in the Campaign Paper, the schedule for visiting each of these places. Tell the dates, time and place. Explain to your church exactly what will be done in each place. Estimate how many Christians will be needed in each group. *Then call for volunteers.*

Make A Study Of The Slum Area.

Make a list of the *rescue missions* in your community. Find out who is in charge of each one. Inquire from them about the different ways they carry on a witness there. Schedule a meeting at the rescue mission for your men during the Week of Visiting.

Try to discover some interesting information about the slum area in your town. Talk with those at the Salvation Army and other similar organizations, about the transients, and the kind of work being done for them. Simply learn all you can about this area of life. Pass it on to your people.

Also, make a list of the "flop houses". (The author knows no other name for them. These are places where the derelict pay 15 cents to 75 cents per night for a cot to sleep on.) Here is one of the most neglected fields in evangelism. Many of these men actually *live* there. Sending Christian laymen to visit in these places can be, and has been, life transforming.

Make A List Of All The Taverns

Draw up a list, with addresses, of all the taverns and "honky tonks", and "pool halls" (billiard clubs!) in your community. Plan to send the men from your church out in pairs one night to visit every one of these places.

(These men do *not* go there and "jump up on a piano and start preaching"! They simply go from table to table, saying, "Good evening, we're out inviting people to visit our church. We'd like for you to read this!" and hand them an evangelistic tract.)

It is amazing the spectacular results of such a simple act. Some of the greatest victories of a Campaign in Personal Evangelism come from Christians passing out tracts in taverns. Very often someone will invite the Christians to sit down and talk to them. The Christian usually discovers the man has come there to drink his troubles away. He is anxious to talk. The most wonderful conversions have often followed.

Even more, though, a Christian is transformed. He is possessed with the most thrilling excitement about the whole thing. The spirit of revival is often born in a church while hearing the testimonies of what God has done through those who have been visiting in these places.

WILL CHRISTIANS GO INTO THESE AREAS?

Pastors often have asked, "But will my people go?"

The question is not "will they go?" The fact is: we have no alternative! If we are to be Christian, we *must* go. Where did we ever get the idea that the church was exempted from these areas anyway? This just happens to be the reason the church is here on this earth in the first place. Every church, from the loftiest Episcopal to the most informal Pentecostal, has a New Testament obligation to go to these areas.

We speak of the "unevangelized areas of the world". We challenge our young people to go there (to foreign fields). The spirit of missions is cultivated at home. We could evangelize the whole world if we would start doing at home what we *expect* on the foreign fields. There is room for "on the job" training here.

Will laymen dare go into these places? The author has been in some of the wealthiest and most reserved churches in every part of America. He has seen millionaires who never even knew these areas existed, go into them and sit down with the "chiefest of sinners". Those Christians have been as transformed as their converts. Christians have returned from these experiences to find a fuller life of witnessing, living, giving and serving.

The author has directed thousands of laymen, some of whom have never been near these places before, to witness in these "unevangelized fields". Not one has ever raised so much as a question. But instead, many have asked, "Why hasn't the church been working in this area before now?"

Remember that Jesus said, "I was in prison and you visited me not. I was hungry and you fed me not. I was naked, and you clothed me not."

The people asked, "Lord, when did we not do these things?"

He answered, "When you did it not to the least of these!"

He added, "Depart from me into everlasting damnation. I never knew you."

What an indictment! These words are aimed at us! Again and again, Jesus hammered away at the theme of the "poor, the halt, the blind, the widowed". He lashed out at the *religious people's neglect*.

Remember that it was *your* Lord who was called a wine bibber and drunkard. A friend of prostitutes. A sinner! If Jesus lived again today, do you really think he would *not* spend most of his time in these same places? His teachings and actions would condemn us today every bit as much as they did the Pharisees then! What a judgment against us all! Oh, the greatest sin of all of us Christians in this age is simply refusal to get our hands dirty!

This author believes that if any pastor in America will stand up in the pulpit and say, "We are going—follow me!" . . . the people will go. Their lives will be transformed. Christianity will have a new meaning. The Church will begin a new day.

Many, many pastors have reported that going to these areas has changed an entire community's attitude toward their church. A whole new image of the church emerges. Suddenly, strangers start calling and asking for counsel. People begin appearing in services who have never even been contacted. A new respect for the church is born. *The lost people of this world seem to sense that "out there" is where Christians should be working.* Rather than being critical, they respect us for daring to come to them. Perhaps the world knows better then we, what we ought to be doing.

It won't be long until words like this may be spoken in the local beer hall: "Preachers are all a bunch of hypocrites, and so are their church members . . ." (This is said every day in such places, so that part is not new.) "That is, except Rev._____of course. Now there's a guy who practices what he believes. I ain't very religious, but if I were, that'd be the kind of church I'd want to go to."

A man of God, a church of God, can receive no higher compliment!

A question: Is it your people, or is it you, who is reluctant to go?

CHAPTER 20

STEP FOUR
SPIRITUAL PREPARATION FOR THE CAMPAIGN

God will meet your church on the level for which it is spiritually prepared. If you do not have spiritual preparation, any efforts to lead your church into a deeper witness will be fruitless.

"All night prayer meetings"; "cottage prayer meetings"; "prayer lists" are all associated with evangelists and great crusades.

One reason *personal* evangelism is so weak in the 20th century is because we never pay the price for it. To win souls, your church will first have to get down on its knees. Reading a book on "How to Win Souls" will not make soul winners any more than reading a book would prepare a church for an evangelist.

Do *not* expect any results at all unless you and your church spend a very great deal of time in prayer.

If anything, personal evangelism demands more spiritual preparation than mass evangelism—certainly not less.

With spiritual preparation, all the power of this universe cannot stop your church from reaching men for Christ.

R. A. Torrey's prescription for revival cannot be improved upon:

> "First, let a few Christians (there may not be many) get thoroughly right with God themselves. This is the prime essential. If this is not done, the rest, I am sorry to say, will come to nothing. Second, let them bind themselves together to pray for revival until God opens the heavens and comes down. Third, let them put themselves at the disposal of God to use them as He sees fit in winning others to Christ. That is all."

Torrey went on to say:

> "This is sure to bring a revival to any church or

community. I have given this prescription around the world. It has been taken by many churches and communities, and in no instance has it ever failed; and it cannot fail."

Preparation for a Campaign in Personal Evangelism will be a unique and exciting experience for your church.

When a church prepares for mass evangelism, it centers its preparation in the church building, because that is where the activities will be. In personal evangelism, the preparation takes place largely in the area of the activity — which is *outside* the church.

PRAYER PREPARATION

Obviously, the greatest spiritual preparation a church can make is through prayer. There should be several groups assigned to the task of preparing for and scheduling prayer meetings. Here's what must be done:

(1) set dates for the prayer meetings
(2) find a *place* for each prayer meeting
(3) place someone in charge of each meeting
(4) publicize and create interest in these meetings.

I.

PRAYER MEETINGS OUTSIDE THE CHURCH

Here are the places where prayer meetings should be scheduled, *outside* the church!

In Homes throughout the Community:

Every community breaks up into natural "neighborhoods". One home should be selected in each neighborhood for a *weekly* prayer meeting. Monday (or Friday) is the best day. There should be one prayer meeting each week for four weeks, in that home. If at all possible, it should be in the same home each week (to avoid changes in announcement of time and place and to avoid the problem of locating a new place each week). It should be left up to the hostess to decide the time of the meeting.

In Factories:

In almost every church, there are several men who work at the same industrial site. There may be several industries where there are enough men from your church to get together once a week for a prayer meeting.

Make a list of all the men who work at the same place. Decide on the dates, time and place of the meeting. Select one man to notify the other men and remind them. He should also be placed in charge of leading the prayer meeting each week.

The prayer meeting should be held at noon during lunch time, if possible. If not, then before work or after work, or at a coffee break. A place may be made available for the meeting by asking the person in charge of "public relations", or simply speaking to the "boss". If there is no place available to meet, the men can always get together in a car. They should feel free to invite other Christian friends who work with them to join them in this prayer meeting.

One primary concern of the meeting should be to pray for the non-Christian men they work with.

There should be at least one meeting per week for four weeks in the factories selected. (Some men may want to meet several times during the week.)

In Office Buildings:

Just as men work in the same industries, business men often work within walking distance of one another in businesses. If possible, arrange for a meeting place somewhere in the business district so that business men and women can meet together for prayer (eg., the conference room of a bank). The meeting should be scheduled at the noon hour.

Other such meetings might be scheduled in other parts of the city.

One man should be in charge. The date, time and place should be well publicized throughout the church.

Prayer Breakfast:

A restaurant can be engaged to serve a (very) early morning breakfast, once each week. The prayer breakfast might serve as a substitute in case factory and business prayer meetings are impossible.

The breakfast should be given over primarily to prayer, and not fellowship. It should meet once a week for four weeks, at the same place, and same hour.

PROMOTING THESE PRAYER MEETINGS

Every effort should be made to get the word out about the prayer meetings. Prepare several large posters, stand them on easels in conspicuous places in your church. They would read, "Attend the Prayer Meeting Nearest You", with a brief word of information on it.

Each week, for 4 weeks *before* the Campaign, these prayer meetings should be publicized in the church bulletin and the campaign paper. The time and place should be printed or mimeographed, and distributed to every member of the church.

Each week, have a report on the attendance, and the results of the prayer meetings.

Everything possible should be done to get the majority of the church membership at one of these meetings each week.

II.

PRAYER IN THE CHURCH

There should be prayer emphases for the Campaign at least once each week for four weeks, *within* the church.

The First Emphasis:

Calling the People Forward.

On Sunday evening, *four* weeks before the Campaign, the pastor might call the congregation to the front of the auditorium for a time of prayer for the Campaign.

The Second Emphasis:

Have a unique Mid-Week Prayer Service.

Most churches have a mid-week service (prayer meeting or Bible study). Here is a unique plan that can be a tremendous blessing.

Have the congregation break up into small groups with five in each group. (Choose a leader beforehand for each group.) After each little group has gathered in various places throughout the auditorium, they should have prayer together. At least 30 minutes of the service should be given over to prayer in this manner.

The Third Emphasis:

Have Mid-Week Services in Homes.

One week before the Campaign, the mid-week prayer service should be dismissed from the church, and meet in homes instead.

By a previously announced schedule, have homes open in every neighborhood in your community. Each family should choose to attend the midweek prayer service in the home nearest them.

These unique "cottage prayer meetings" often become unusual spiritual blessings.

(No refreshments should be served.)

HOW TO PRAY

The author would like to suggest the method of prayer. (Unwittingly, we do employ certain "methods" of prayer.) A very refreshing approach to these prayer meetings in homes, offices, factories, can be suggested.

Here is the way most groups pray: Each person prays, taking turns, praying around a circle. The first prayer is usually long and inclusive. Then each person prays until everyone has prayed once, and the prayer meeting is over.

Here is a suggestion that lends itself far better to group prayer :

Do not pray around the circle. Rather, follow no sequence at all. Do not pray long prayers. Instead, let as many as wish pray a *very brief* prayer. No one should pray over *one* minute. No one should pray about more than one subject at any one time. Then, without following any order (two or three people may pray "back and forth" several times), let each person pray again as a request comes to mind.

This way, the Holy Spirit has more freedom to prompt each person. Each Christian's mind is constantly active and does not wander, (as it will when there is nothing to do but listen to someone else praying a long prayer.)

Suggest it. Try it.

(A good time to introduce this concept is on the night you have the congregation break up into small prayer groups throughout the auditorium.)

OTHER SPIRITUAL PREPARATION

The pulpit should be a cry for evangelism. Every organization should place emphasis on witnessing. Every prayer uttered should include it. Each Sunday School teacher should emphasize it. Devotionals should be prepared on this subject, and given at each gathering.

If your church has (or can have) a "testimonial time", then plan to give time for Christians to tell about past experiences in personal witnessing, and answered prayer.

PREPARE A SPECIAL SUNDAY SCHOOL LESSON

On the Sunday that the Campaign begins, every Sunday School class should be studying a specially-created lesson on "Personal Evangelism In the New Testament Church". This lesson must be prepared at least four weeks before the Campaign. It must be printed or mimeographed. It needs to be passed out in all Sunday School classes on the two Sundays before it is studied in class, so everyone will have plenty of time to study it.

The pastor, because of the spiritual nature of the lesson, and because there will be no teacher's manual to receive helps from, will need to teach the lesson to all the teachers.

The lesson can be based on the Book of Acts. (See "A Look At New Testament Evangelism," Chapter 5.) Or it can be a discussion of Luke 14:16ff.

The pastor should prepare the lesson. A word about evangelizing the world . . . going to our "Jerusalem" . . . and the similarity between this Campaign and the ministry of the Disciples, might well be discussed.

Make the lesson strongly Bible based, so it can be a truly significant experience to all who study it.

EMPHASIZE THE SPIRIT FILLED LIFE

Soul winning and the *fulness* of the Spirit of God go hand in hand. Not only must the pastor be Spirit filled, and even more, *walking* in the Spirit of God — but so must his people.

Here is a subject to be preached on and taught. Clearly show, from God's Word, how a Christian can have this experience for his own life. Call your people to the experience.

Expect God to meet you, and move upon your church and anoint it for the task ahead, just as He did His first disciples.

CHAPTER 21

STEP FIVE
THE WEEK OF TRAINING

"I don't see how you can keep from running out of something to say." This was one pastor's reaction as he thought about spending 7 days in soul winning training. Really, 7 days are hardly enough . . . and the training must be very intense.

The Campaign begins on Sunday. It is a two week meeting. The *Week of Training* gets underway the day the campaign begins. The first training session, which will be introductory, should begin on Sunday evening, an hour before the Sunday evening worship service.

There should be a session each night Monday through Friday. Take Saturday off. Then there should be one last practice session again the next Sunday evening.

HOW TO PREPARE FOR THE WEEK OF TRAINING

Decide on the *place* in your church building where the training sessions should be held. Usually the auditorium is best. If you have a very large and comfortable room somewhere else in the building, you might decide to use it, to avoid the atmosphere of worship that the sanctuary sometimes creates.

The platform should not be obstructed by a large pulpit. At the most, use only a small music stand. There should be three or four chairs on the platform, or perhaps two chairs and a sofa. Some churches like to go all the way, with an entire living room scene. Though effective, this is certainly not essential.

Be sure to have your *prospect cards* and your *visitation packets* all ready before the Week of Training begins. You will want to explain them and show them to your people. Have a large number of *New Testaments* on hand. The majority of the people will want one.

Because you will want to teach soul winning in a very conversational tone, and not in a loud voice, and because you will be moving about as you teach, a lapel *microphone* is almost indispensable (if the room is large).

The service should consist of only one song and a prayer. Go right into the training session. Try to have two 45 minute sessions each evening, with a five-minute break in between. (You may find the five minute break unnecessary, if the interest is keen, because there is always a lot of audience "action".)

You will want to select someone to be your "dummy" during the week of training. This is the man you will ask to play the part of the lost person in all your demonstrations.

You will need a *textbook*. Every person in the campaign will need his own copy. Over and over every night, you should emphasize the need of everyone reading the dialogue aloud each day. In the back of this book is a bibliography of a few books that have been written on soul winning from a new vantage point. Pick the one that suits you best.

Remember, you as instructor, must have mastered the plan completely at least three or four months before the Campaign. If you know the plan and have won souls to Christ with it, you will be able to teach it easily.

Study again the chapter on "A New Concept in Soul Winning Training."

SCHEDULE FOR THE WEEK OF TRAINING

Sunday Evening Session:

1. Begin the session by asking, "What are the things that keep us from being soul winners?"
   (Get plenty of answers from the audience.)

2. Point out that the main reason is FEAR. Fear is caused by not knowing how to witness.

3. Explain that soul winning falls into three phases: (1) beginning; (2) presenting Jesus Christ as the way of salvation; (3) the decision.

4. Explain the problems of beginning. (Fear on your part; resentment from the lost person; not being able to tell whether a person is saved or lost by the answers he gives.)

5. Present the principle which remove these three problems — working with the Holy Spirit.

6. Illustrate Jesus talking to the woman at the well, and Nicodemus.

7. Explain the principle of beginning a soul winning conversation gradually.

8. Explain the reasons every "beginner" needs a plan. Illustrate the effectiveness of a plan.

9. Introduce the plan which will be used.

10. Present the text book.

11. Dismiss with prayer.

Monday Session:

(A song and a prayer)

1. Begin the first part of the Monday night session by teaching the *Art of Visiting**.

   Explain that the church will follow a new procedure in visitation. Explain the "visitation service" and the mechanics of visitation (See Chapter 23, "The Visitation Program"). Then illustrate the visitation service (a song, a prayer; five cards and why; the visitation packet and how to use it; going in pairs and why; the stewardship of cards; explain the U.S. postal card idea; how to leave the church; what to do in the car; returning after visiting; and how to fill out cards.)

2. Explain and demonstrate what to do when you leave the church with your cards and go to the car:

---

* *Here's How To Win Souls,* by Gene Edwards.

(1) Arrange the cards geographically
(2) Decide who will be the soul winner. (The other will be the silent partner.)
(3) Have prayer
(4) Check your equipment
(5) Memorize the name listed on the first card.

3. Explain and illustrate what to do when the couple arrives at the home and gets out of the car.
   (1) Don't talk
   (2) Observe the yard for information about the family.

4. Explain — and demonstrate — *What to do at the Door*.
   (1) Knock. Step back. (Emphasize the need of a smile.)
   (2) The caller's first words. (Have audience repeat over and over.)
   (3) Demonstrate what to do:
      (a) If a woman comes to the door (when men are visiting).
      (b) If the husband is not home.
      (c) If you are not invited in. (Ask for best time to come back, etc.)
      (d) If no one is home. (Leave church publicity on the door.)
   (4) Explain, and demonstrate, how to get in the home. (May we come in and visit for a few . . .)

5. Explain and demonstrate *What to do when You walk into the home*.
   (1) Be friendly. Introduce yourself to everyone.
   (2) Find something to compliment.
   (3) Get the TV off. (Audience repeats exact words.)

6. Explain the General Conversation — *The First 10 Minutes In the Home*.
   (1) Tell Christians exactly what to talk about.
   (2) Warning: Keep the conversation general!

(3) Don't wait too long to begin witnessing!

(4) Don't talk about church membership!
(Stress each of these points. They are very important!)

7. Now call for questions from the audience. Discuss all the problems that are brought up. Have the audience repeat again, exactly what to say at the door; and what to say to get the TV off.

8. Now take up the DUTIES OF THE SILENT PARTNER.
Explain all his duties; demonstrate each duty (especially how to ask for a drink of water).

DUTIES OF THE SILENT PARTNER ARE:

(1) Be silent.

(2) Look interested.

(3) Pray.

(4) Baby sit.

(5) Run interference (get thirsty).

(6) Get the soul winner and lost person seated together.

(7) Strengthen the decision.

9. If you have time for the Approach Steps, simply review "the problems and principles of beginning". Begin teaching the use of the (six) approach steps.

10. As you close the Monday evening session, have everyone commit themselves to study the soul winning plan before they go to bed tonight.

Tuesday Session:

Tuesday evening is primarily for mastering the art of beginning a soul winning conversation (the approach steps). Emphasize the work of the Holy Spirit in soul winning. Then explain the advantages of having a plan to work from.

1. Explain how to use *Step One* ("Do you ever give much thought to spiritual things?")

    (1) If there is a Bible or religious picture in the room.

    (2) If there is no Bible or picture. Teach them to begin by saying, "Bill since you have been living here, have you and your wife given much thought . . . or talked about . . . your spiritual needs?"

2. Explain and demonstrate how to witness relaxed and natural. (This needs to be emphasized and demonstrated clearly.)

3. Explain how to "go to the next question". The (six) steps are designed in such a way that regardless of the answer, you can always move on to the next question.

4. Explain and illustrate questions *two and three*. Emphasize the need of moving slowly, and not getting ahead of the Holy Spirit.

5. Explain the most important step of all: "In your opinion, what would you say a person has to do to be a Christian?"

    (1) The answer will tell you if the person is saved.

    (2) You don't have to ask him directly; yet he tells you, and without knowing he told you.

    (3) Whenever you go to a home, never assume that anyone is either lost or saved. By asking this question, *discover* which is true. (Be sure to record your findings when you report your visit on the back side of the prospect card.)

6. Explain and demonstrate the rest of the steps. (How to get the Bible open.)

7. Now break the entire audience up into pairs.
    (1) Have the audience repeat the (six) questions in unison.
    (2) Then have each pair to turn and ask one another the questions.

8. Explain what to do if someone refuses to let you read the Scriptures. Explain what to do if someone says he does not believe the Bible.

9. Now demonstrate how to "Present Christ" with the four Scripture verses. Go through the entire plan. Ask for questions from the audience.

10. Urge everyone to continue studying. Dismiss the service.

Wednesday Session

1. Begin with a quick five minute review of:
   (1) The visitation service (outline it step by step).
   (2) The stewardship of cards.
   (3) The Art of Visiting. (Outline.)

2. Have a three minute review of how to begin a soul winning conversation. Repeat the approach steps, together, aloud.

3. Explain the problems of trying to witness with proof text, argument and verses. Explain how to present the plan of salvation by working with the Holy Spirit. Explain how to eliminate excuses by lifting up Jesus Christ, rather than answering them.

4. Have the entire audience open their Bibles and read the four Scriptures. (This is so everyone gets practice in opening their Bible, finding the Scriptures, and reading them aloud.)

5. Repeat the process again, only on the second practice, add the "connecting sentences", or "bridge sentences" (key thoughts).

6. Demonstrate the entire plan again with your "dummy". Only this time, interrupt yourself as you go along, explaining why and how to do certain things. Put emphasis on explaining how to press for a decision.

As you close, urge everyone to study dilligently.

Thursday Evening

Begin by quickly reviewing the entire steps in the Art of Visiting. Repeat the Approach Steps. Then have everyone read the four Scriptures aloud.

1. Discuss exactly how to press for a decision. Demonstrate this part very mechanically. Cover every detail, for "drawing the net" is the most important of all.

2. Have the audience split up into pairs. Then go through the plan. Have the audience to repeat with you the highlights and key sentences in the plan.

3. Call for questions and answers. There should be several questions.

4. Now let each pair ask one another the approach steps. Instruct them to read the four Scriptures to one another and try to remember to put in the "connecting sentences" between verses.

(This is not a real soul winning practice session. Instead of going through the plan, each person simply goes through the skeleton, or outline, of the plan with one another.)

Friday Evening

Begin by calling for questions from the audience. Quickly review the entire plan, in outline form, so that it is fresh in everyone's mind. Then split the entire audience into two's. Let them scatter throughout the auditorium.

Here are some suggestions:

Every person is to go through the entire plan. No cheating, no one can peek at the textbook. The Christian who first plays the part of the "lost person" is to be very cooperative, and simply answer "yes" or "no", as the soul winner speaks to him. Tell him to keep in mind that just as soon as he is "won", he has to swap around with his partner and do the part of the soul winner.

Emphasize that everyone is to go all the way through the plan, and especially, not to leave out the moment of decision.

If anyone forgets what to say next, just stop and think. Go to the next thing in the plan that comes to mind. (Remember you can't ask your partner, the "lost person". He doesn't know, being "lost".)

Encourage the audience by reminding them, "Tonight will be the worst job of witnessing you'll ever do! You will never be as poor again as you are going to be tonight. It is better to do a poor job of witnessing tonight, while practicing on a sympathetic Christian, than to do so on a person who truly needs Christ."

While the group is practicing, walk up and down the aisles, and give assistance where it is needed. When the practice session is over and *everyone* in the room has "witnessed to and won" someone to Christ, then have a question and answer period.

Now do one last thing, but be sure and wait UNTIL FRIDAY night. Explain the *limitations* of a plan:

(1) Never force a witness. Just repeating a plan to someone will never win them to Chriist.

(2) Always, when you are beginning the witness, stop if you meet with resentment.

(3) Bring a witness to a close, right in the middle of the plan, when you can definitely tell that the Holy Spirit is not creating interest and bringing conviction.

(4) The plan is designed to be used "as if it were the only way in the world to win souls." Use it, word for word, until you have won ten people to

Christ. By then, you will have lost your fear and gained real wisdom and experience from the Holy Spirit. After that, you're on your own.

Now take a moment to explain again what will be happening next week, during the WEEK OF VISITING. Remind everyone there will be no Saturday session. There will be one more practice session on Sunday evening.

Sunday Evening Session:

The Sunday evening session should be just like the Friday evening session. The entire session would be given over to practicing the plan. You will be amazed at how perfectly everyone will be able to practice the plan in this session. This is the "breakthrough" session, when everyone realizes that they really can witness.

Very often, a Christian will win someone to Christ during the Week of Training. If so, have them stand and give their testimony.

(Many churches have actually dismissed the Sunday evening worship service, and started the Week of *Visiting* on this Sunday evening.)

THE WEEK OF VISITING GETS UNDERWAY TOMORROW!

CHAPTER 22

STEP SIX

THE WEEK OF VISITING

One entire week of soul winning visitation can prove to be the greatest hour in the history of a church. This week must be preceded by weeks of preparation, as well as a very thorough Week of Training. When the Week of Visiting is over, it must be followed immediately by a regular weekly visitation program.

The Week of Visiting should begin on Monday night, after the Week of Training has ended on Sunday evening. There should be visitation every morning and every evening, Monday through Friday.

The Week of Visiting must follow a prescribed plan of action. This plan must be worked out in detail weeks before. The schedule of the week's activities needs to be published for at least three weeks ahead of time. This schedule needs to appear in the bulletin, the campaign paper, and should be discussed during the Week of Training. Everyone in the church must be fully familiar with its purpose.

During the Week of Visiting, Christians will be doing two kinds of witnessing: (1) evangelism in institutions, and (2) house to house evangelism.

INSTITUTIONAL VISITING

This is a ministry of visiting hospitals, old folks homes, colleges, dormitories, etc. It also includes the more dramatic challenges, such as the jail, tavern, the rescue mission, etc.*

This type of witnessing takes planning and scheduling.

A different group of Christians must be assigned to each one of these places. Some of the groups will need to plan

* See chapter entitled "Survey the Neglected Areas of your Community"

a program (eg., old folks home). Everyone in the church will want to know where he will be going and the exact time and place.

Most "institutional" witnessing should be done on Monday and Tuesday. (A man who has passed out tracts in a tavern on Monday, finds that witnessing in a home on Wednesday is mild!)

Here is a suggested schedule:

Monday Morning and AFTERNOON:

Schedule as much group visitation as possible on Monday mornings and afternoons. Send the ladies out to these prearranged places (hospitals, homes for unwed mothers, womens wards in the jail, old folks home, etc.)

On Tuesday morning, *begin* the regular "house to house" evangelism, and *finish* any institutional visitation not done on Monday.

Monday and Tuesday EVENING:

Some house to house visitation should be planned on Monday night for the ladies who attend. The men, though, should go out in a spectacular thrust of witnessing in the "highways and hedges".

(Re-read the chapters on "Plan the Campaign" and "Survey the Neglected Areas", for more details.)

On Tuesday *evening*, round out any places that were not visited on Monday evening.

It is needless to say that the pastor will have to lead out in this daring visitation. The men will follow, and it will turn out to be one of the most delightful experiences of a lifetime.

HOUSE TO HOUSE EVANGELISM

From Tuesday through Friday, most of the witnessing will be done from house to house. The next chapter, "A Visitation Program", tells the exact schedule to follow each night and morning during the Week of Visiting.

The only alteration to be made in the program during the Week of Visiting, that is different than what is described in the next chapter, is this: all the prospect cards used during the Week of Visiting should be *evangelistic prospects* and *newcomers*. Make *only* evangelistic visits during the Campaign.

A Schedule to follow:

Here is an outline of how to carry out visitation each day during the entire week. It is described in detail in the next chapter. The procedure will be identical for morning and evening visitation.

Start on time.

Have one song and a prayer and a few words of instruction.

Pass out the cards: each couple gets five.

Pick up the Visitation Packet.

Go to the cars.

After about one and a half hours of visiting:

Return to the church.

Fill out, in detail, a report on each visit, on the back of the prospect card.

Have a time of testimonial and report.

Go home.

Saturday Follow Up

When the week is over, the pastor and the staff, along with a group of key laymen, should spend all day Saturday following up those who made decisions in the home during the week. Go see every person, congratulate them on their decision, invite them to come to church tomorrow; find out if they have transportation; get them committed to come.

A successful week of soul winning visitation will always reap a thrilling Sunday morning harvest, when *follow up* is added.

Saturday Night for Young People:

Some churches have planned a special kind of visitation for the young people on Saturday night, if there is a rural area nearby. The young people go out and visit all the farming families. This rounds out, "in the streets and lanes of the cities . . . into the highways, and *hedges*".

Sunday Afternoon:

Plan to end the Week of Visiting by sending your people out on Sunday afternoon. Finish out any "institutional visitation" that was not done last Monday and Tuesday; all homes that have been missed up until now, and continue follow up on those who were converted in the homes.

Climaxing the Week:

On Sunday evening, throw the service open to testimonials of the week. Give everyone who participated an opportunity to tell their experiences. Let those who did not participate, hear what they missed. Let everyone thrill to the power of God in the lives of men.

Close with a brief evangelistic message, and as in the morning service, give those who were won to Christ in the homes an opportunity to make their decision public.

Take time to praise, and give God the glory!

When this week is over, you have laid the foundation for a permanent program of visitation and for SUSTAINED EVANGELISM. You have taken the first step in becoming a soul winning church.

Now get ready to move into a regular, weekly, evangelistic visitation program.

CHAPTER 23

STEP SEVEN
THE VISITATION PROGRAM*

Just as soon as the Campaign in Personal Evangelism is over, start a weekly visitation program. The whole Campaign has been aimed at "breaking the ground" and laying a foundation for a weekly program of evangelism in the church. Perhaps for the first time in the history of the church, it will actually be *ready* for a visitation program. Actually, the Christians who participated in the Campaign will be eager to begin a weekly program of personal evangelism. The whole atmosphere and attitude of the church toward visitation should be transformed by now.

You have the *foundation* for building a sustained program of soul winning in your church. Now lay the first *brick*: a weekly visitation program!

SET SOME STANDARDS

Choose A Day

Pick one day out of the week, which the members of your church will spend in visitation. One day a week for winning souls is the absolute minimum that any church can afford. This day is usually referred to as "Visitation Day". Many churches have discovered it to be more effective to call it *"Evangelism Day"*.

You must carve one day of the week right out of the life of the church, and put it in a complete vacuum. Have it understood that absolutely no activities, no class parties, nor any other kind of meetings, can take place on Evangelism Day. This is the day the church wins souls.

This day has only one purpose — the ministry of soul winning through visitation. That means that "Evangelism Day" cannot be the day the choir meets; it cannot be the

---

* Use the information covered in this chapter as a guide during the Week of Visiting.

day committees meet; or when the women's missionary organization meets. This cannot be youth night. This cannot be the *pastor's day off!* This cannot be the day the church puts out the bulletin or newsletter. This cannot be a day when the pastor is scheduled for counseling or for committee meetings.

Also, Evangelism Day should be as permanent a part of your church's life as is the Sunday Morning Worship Service. You do not discontinue 11:00 worship service a dozen times a year. You cannot call off "Evangelism Day" for other activities, either. You should plan your calendar so as to have "Evangelism Day" at least 50 weeks per year!

How to Choose A Day.

The best day for "Evangelism Day" is usually Thursday (it's close to the next Sunday); or Monday (it's close to last Sunday). It might be best to start on Thursday and continue using this day for at least one *year*. Then shift to Monday. Every church is different, as is every community. Some other night might be ideal. Some churches have actually turned the mid-week services exclusively into "house to house" evangelism.

A BIRD'S EYE VIEW OF "EVANGELISM DAY"

Let's imagine that you have picked Thursday as Evangelism Day. There should be a visitation program in the morning and then one in the evening. (Or else one in the afternoon, and one that evening.) About an hour before Visitation begins, the pastor should sit down with the cards, pull out evangelistic prospects, and arrange them for visitation. (Here's a hint: turn the box around backwards and examine the reports on the back side of the cards. This is the quickest way to locate the best cards for visitation.) Begin on time. Then the pastor assigns the prospect cards he has selected to each couple, and sends them out — "two by two".

Everyone is to return to the church at the end of their

visits. Each pair should sit down and write out a report of the visit on the back of the cards, and return the cards to the pastor.

The morning visitation should begin about 9:30 a.m., and finish about 11:00 a.m. (This gives the ladies just enough time to prepare lunch for their husbands.)

The evening visitation service should be scheduled something like 7:00 to 8:45 p.m.

> Note: It will be necessary that the Nursery be open in the morning and the evening, if you expect to have a large turn out of young adults.

Do not encourage — rather discourage — your visitation program from becoming divided into women visiting in the morning and men in the evening. You should encourage all the men possible to attend the morning visitation service, and all the women possible to attend the evening visitation service.

What About Meals:

Many churches wonder about the merit of having a luncheon for those who visit in the morning, and/or having an evening meal for those who go visiting in the evening. One thing has been clearly proven: churches that serve an evening meal for workers find great success in keeping their visitation program going. Nonetheless, this is a decision that you will have to make on your own, according to the background of the church and the convictions of the pastor. (Downtown churches in big cities will find it almost an absolute necessity to serve a meal, because of the distance the people must travel.)

Now that we have taken a "bird's eye view" of the visitation program, let's take a closer look at the details of its functions and why these details are all so necessary.

THE PASTOR MUST BE IN CHARGE

There is only one person who should prepare the cards for visitation. That one person is the *pastor*. Some pastors have a layman in the church to do this. But the pastor knows the people of the community better than anyone else. He also needs to keep up with what is happening to people in the community. He is the only one qualified to decide who should go visit whom. He knows the people in his church best, and which ones are best suited to visit certain prospects. Also much of the information that workers write on the back of cards after their visit in a home, will be important to the pastor, and he will want to direct certain actions regarding it.

If a pastor will not prepare the cards and be in charge of visitation, then he can give up the idea of having an evangelistic church. The pastor must attend visitation just like everyone else. If he doesn't, there won't be any visitation. And, of course, if he attends, he will take charge of the visitation procedures and furnish the leadership image that he alone can give.

Any pastor who lets someone else be in charge of the visitation program has doomed it before it has started. A strong visitation program cannot survive without the pastor leading it. The pastor *must* attend every visitation service, and go visiting with his people when they do.

Preparing the Cards for Visitation:

The best way to prepare the cards for visitation is for the pastor to arrive an hour before visitation begins, and go through the prospect file box. Arrange the cards in stacks of fives.*

Put them out neatly on a table. Keep the file of women prospects on one side (five cards in each stack) and keep the prospects for men on the other side. As you arrange

---

* *Why five cards?* If you give each pair just two or three cards, most of them will be back to church in 30 minutes saying, "no one was home". If you give each pair four cards, most of them will find someone at home, but one or two workers will come back saying no one was home. If you give each pair five cards, the law of averages will guarantee that everyone finds someone at home.

Giving each pair five cards does not mean that each pair is expected to make five visits. One or two visits will be maximum in one night.

the cards, keep in mind who your workers are. You will want the cards to be arranged pretty much by age. If you have a church with a lot of young Christians, then you will want to try to match the prospects according to age. All of the older prospects you will want to keep separated to give to your older Christian workers who come to the visitation service.

Also keep in mind the kind of workers you have, as you arrange your cards. You may even arrange each stack of cards with certain people in mind. Some of the workers in your church will be better qualified to visit in one area of town than some others might be.

Keep the cards arranged geographically. It is best to set the prospect file system up by streets. It is easy for you to pull the cards out of the box by streets. If you will keep your cards arranged this way, when you pull them out of the file box, Christian workers will be able to visit all evening without getting off one street or leaving one area.

There are several ways that you can arrange these five cards:

1. In each stack of five cards, you can place two evangelistic prospects: two newcomers; and one or two church prospects.

2. There will be times when you will notice that your newcomers cards are piling up on you. When your visitation program is not keeping up with all newcomers moving into the community, give each couple five newcomer prospect cards.

3. There may be times, before an evangelistic campaign perhaps, when you will want to give out only evangelistic prospects. This should be done from time to time anyway, just to make sure that each Christian is given an *unavoidable opportunity* to witness.

How to use the Visitation Packet:

In Chapter 18, ("Plan the Campaign") we talked about the Visitation Packet. This is an indispensable tool to the "Week of Visiting", and to your regular visitation program.

Here is what to tell your people about using the Visitation Packet.

1. Church Publicity

   Church publicity should be left at every home, regardless of what kind of visit is made. Leave *church publicity* at the door when no one is home. In this way, the workers never "lose" a visit. The family will always know that they had church callers while they were out.

2. Blank Census Card.

   Very often, workers will visit a home and discover that the prospect has moved away, and a new family has moved in. The workers will want to go into the home anyway and meet the *newcomers*. While visiting this new family, the worker can take a *census card* out of the packet and fill in the information about the family.

3. Evangelistic Tracts.

   Evangelistic tracts should be given to those who are witnessed to but who do not receive Christ as their Saviour.

4. Literature for New Converts *(1 John)*

   Every new convert who is won to Christ ought to have something given to him to read when he is converted.

5. A Map of the Community.

   Each Packet should have a map of the community. In this way, the workers can quickly locate streets and houses. (Never take it for granted that the members of your church are familiar with your town, no matter how small. They are not!)

(It should be the church secretary's job to keep the packets filled and ready for use each week.)

HOW TO CONDUCT THE VISITATION SERVICE

The key to effective visitation is *punctuality* and *discipline*. The Christian workers who come to pick up prospect cards must have confidence in the visitation program. The worker must feel that he is not wasting his time — that the pastor is interested, and that he has made preparation — that the cards are accurate, and that there will be needy people to be visited.

Here is an outline of a visitation service:

1. Start On Time.

   Even if you have only enough people present for one or two pairs, start on time. Don't wait for others to show up. If you do, your visitation will begin later and later every week until finally it loses all purpose.

2. Have a Song and a Prayer.

   Have just one song. Do not have an elaborate service. One song and a brief prayer will be best. Remember that most of the praying will be done in the cars after each couple leaves the church.

   (Do not have a devotional or Scripture lesson.)

3. Have a Moment of Instruction.

   Take a moment to instruct your workers. The instruction period will vary each week. The first few times you will need to explain the use of the Visitation Packet. Sometimes you will be reminding the workers of their need of writing clear reports of their visits. Remind them to return the cards. Instruct them on what to do if they cannot return to the church after visitation. (Explain the use of the return postal cards.)

   At different times of the year, you will have different emphases in your church. This includes Vacation Bible School, the coming evangelistic campaign, the Christmas music program, and other activities that come at different times of the year.

Use the time of instruction to remind everyone of the importance of a *first visit* to a family. Explain over and over how to *discover* if the prospect is really a Christian, or perhaps a lost church member, etc. Remind them to *write out* what they discover *on the back of the card.*

All future visits made to that home will have to depend on the information that you, the church visitor, write on the back of the card.

4. Hand Out the Cards.

Ask everyone to stand and have them to come forward. They should stand to your left, near the table where you have the cards laid out. The pastor alone decides who gets what cards.*

You may want to pair off the first few people yourself, by calling their names. Usually the others will choose partners and will be paired off by the time they reach you. Don't hesitate to re-shuffle any pairs, according to your wishes. Be sure everyone gets a Visitation Packet.

It is the pastor's privilege to split a pair at any time he wants to rearrange couples for more effective visiting, or to provide transportation for each couple.

As you send them out of the room, keep about 20 feet between each pair. They are to go immediately to their cars. No one should be allowed to stop or congregate in the church, talking to one another.

---

* Never let the workers pick their own cards for visiting. Most Christians, when left to do this, will either go visit absentees, or call on church prospects, or pick out the very easiest calls possible. It is just human nature to try to avoid the intimate soul winning visit that is so necessary and important to be made. Also, if the Christian workers choose their own cards, then some prospects will get visited many times, and others will be neglected. A church's program of evangelism cannot be built on such hit and miss methods.

5. Returning to the Church.

About an hour and a half after visitation began, the pastor should return to the church from *his* visiting just a *little* earlier than the rest, to be on hand when the other workers begin coming back. As they come in, he should meet them, listen to their stories, give encouragement and advice. Rejoice with the happy, encourage the disappointed.

Each pair should sit down and write a brief report of their visits. Many of them will want to say something personal to the pastor about the visit. The cards should be returned neatly to the table in stacks of five. Before the evening is over, the pastor should return the cards to the box. (It is best to send the workers home *without* any *refreshments*. Refreshment periods after visitation each week can sometimes turn into social events, and before you know it, the tail is wagging the dog.)

Send everyone home very quickly. Do not let anyone remain to "fellowship". (In this way, no one can complain about having to be out late.)

It may be wisest not to have a report after visitation. Save these reports to be given publicly in the church on Sunday night, so that the rest of the church can hear about the results. This way, the entire church hears about visitation. This can help promote interest throughout the church.

THE STEWARDSHIP OF PROSPECT CARDS
(How to Get the Cards Back)

Most churches are plagued with the problem of "How do I get the cards back?" This is a problem that just must be solved. There is too much wasted energy having a secretary type cards every week. The loss of the cards means a loss of prospects. The greatest tragedy of all is the loss of the record of the visits. It is absolutely necessary that the record of visits be preserved.

HOW?

Here is a very simple program that, if followed, will prevent the loss of even *one* card.

1. Never let prospect cards out of the church except on Evangelism Day. Do not let the cards out on that day, *except* through the regular visitation service.

2. Do not let anyone take cards out unless they are coming back to the church within the next two hours. If a couple going visiting cannot return to the church after visitation is over, then do not let them have the cards!

3. Here is a simple program for those who want to visit, but who cannot return to the church after visitation:

    Hand the worker the visitation cards and a U. S. postal card. (Have the church's address stamped on the postal card.) Let the workers copy the information off the prospect card onto the United States Postal Card. The workers can then take the postal cards with them on their visit instead of the prospect cards. The prospect cards stay at the church. When the workers have finished their visiting, they can write a summary of the visits made, onto the postal card; the postal card can be dropped in a mail box on the way home, and it will arrive at the church office the next day. The secretary can record the results of the visits on the prospect card.

    This way, the element of chance is removed. Cards just don't get lost.

4. If a Christian comes to the church during the middle of the week and wants to go visiting, repeat the postal card process. Instead of giving him the prospect cards, give him a postal card. He can copy the information off the prospect cards onto the postal

card and mail the postal card back to the church when he is through visiting.

(This system has been used in churches all over America, and has proven to be 100 per cent effective.)

By following the procedure set forth in this chapter during the Week of Visiting, your people will have the church's new pattern of visitation firmly in mind. By continuing it immediately thereafter in the weekly visitation program, it becomes a natural part of their lives.

In the next chapter we will learn how to sustain the soul winning visitation emphasis . . . and how to bring Christians to the point that they are witnessing every day, wherever they are, as a natural part of their lives.

HOW TO KEEP YOUR CARD FILE UP TO DATE
(Have your Secretary read this section)

What makes cards get out of date? Only one thing: people moving out of houses. In order to keep your cards up to date, all you need to do is to make a personal visit to *every newcomer* who moves into your community.

So your first, and most important, step is to get a "Newcomers List". In some cities, this is called "Welcome Wagon", "Welcome Service", "Credit Stimulator", "Welcome Hostess". Virtually every town and city in America compiles a list of newcomers. Most of the cities make this information available to churches. This information can sometimes be secured through the Chamber of Commerce, or through professional organizations that compile such lists.

> Note: There are other sources, in case these fail. Funeral homes, county court houses, and large business concerns. In rare instances, you may have someone in your church who works for the telephone company, the gas company, or the post office, who can supply you with this information.

The Newcomers List will usually cost your church a few dollars per month. It is one of the most valuable investments a church can make.

Now how can you use your Newcomers List to keep your prospect file up to date?

First, remember that if your religious census was 100 per cent complete, then you have a card for every house and for every family who lives in your community.

Next:

Once a week, the church secretary can take the Newcomers List and compare the addresses of these newcomers with the same addresses in the prospect file. The church secretary can remove the cards which correspond to the addresses of newcomers.

The secretary should not throw the cards away just yet. It could be that the Newcomers List is inaccurate.

The secretary should now take a blank census card and clip it to the card she has removed from the file. On the blank card she should write down the name and address of the newcomers. She should give both cards to the pastor. He, in turn, should give the cards out to the workers on Visitation Day.

The Christian workers can then make a "Newcomers visit": go to the address, find out if a newcomer really has moved in. If so, visit the newcomer. Try to find out if the newcomers are Christians. If the newcomer is lost, the Christian worker should seek to win him to Christ. If the newcomer is a Christian, then the worker should attempt to bring this Christian into the church.

The Christian should then report back to the church. The card on the newcomer should be turned over to the pastor. The pastor will then unclip the old card and destroy it. In its place he will drop the new card into the prospect file box.

By following this process on every newcomer who moves into the community, you can keep your prospect file 100 per cent accurate and 100 per cent up to date.

Note: The author has watched many churches grow to the point that they could keep up with every "newcomer" into the community, all other known prospects, all visitors to the church on Sunday, *plus* a seasonal emphasis on absentees.

A WORD ABOUT ABSENTEE VISITATION

Absentee visitation should never be done on the regular day for visitation. A church that tries to spread its energies to cover not only evangelistic prospects, church prospects, and newcomers, but *also* tries to cover *absentees* will *destroy* its visitation program.

There are two ways that *absentees* can be handled:

1. Once every three or four months, have an all-out effort in absentee visitation.
2. Leave absentee visitation to the teachers; they should contact their absentees throughout the week—NOT during regular visitation.

For a church to concentrate on absentee visitation is the crime of attending to one sheep when the ninety and nine are lost.

If a church will make soul winning the heart and core of visitation, then the fire it creates and the results it engenders will allow you to build other kinds of visitation around this nucleus. But if you place *first* emphasis on any other kind of visitation and try to substitute it as the heart of the visitation program, the visitation program will suffer, and eventually die.

A WORD TO RURAL PASTORS ABOUT VISITATION

The author was once pastor of a rural church in a community of about 200 people. I had done everything to lead my people into becoming an evangelistic church. In spite of all my efforts, neither I nor the church made any progress. I asked one of the greatest soul winners in the world this question: "I have a rural church. How can I get my people to win souls?"

His answer, at the time, was crushing. It was later to have a profound effect on my life. Here is what he said:

"Don't try to make your church into a soul winning church. Forget the idea. You can do all the soul winning there ever needs to be done in your community."

I was puzzled and dismayed. Later, I came to realize that I wanted my people to win souls because I was afraid to do it alone! I went back to my church and tried it — alone! I will not guarantee that what happend to my church will happen to yours, but within a few months, after a profound change came over *this pastor*, my people began to win souls, too.

Let this advice be passed on to every rural pastor: Go win those souls yourself. That's the important thing.

CHAPTER 24

THE SCIENCE OF SUSTAINED EVANGELISM

There is a science to sustaining evangelism in your church. It is possible to have a church in which:

"The Lord added to the church daily."

Remember, the way to *sustain* personal evangelism is first to *start* it!

I have seen many churches come out of a Campaign in Personal Evangelism, to go on to grow a bigger weekly visitation program and consistently win more to Christ than they did in the Campaign itself. Many churches have grown visitation programs almost as large as their Sunday evening congregations.

As has already been suggested, as soon as the Campaign has ended, move immediately into "Sustained Evangelism". The first thing to do is begin a weekly visitation program.

What comes next? You should have a year's *Calendar of Personal Evangelism* planned. When the Campaign is over, begin following this calendar immediately. (You should draw up your year's Calendar of Personal Evangelism as soon as you have finished this book.)

Some of the points discussed in this chapter can be considered simply as *suggestions*. Others you will find are *indispensable* if you are to continue personal evangelism in your church.

I. THE KEY TO SUSTAINED EVANGELISM

The key to keeping evangelism is *continued training*.

Plan another Soul Winning Campaign in the next six months!

Don't expect *one* campaign to be a cure-all for the next decade. You have one or two evangelists in your church each year. You never expect them to establish permanent results! They do not set in motion a program of mass evangelism which lasts 365 days a year. They do not sustain revival. But you keep having evangelistic campaigns.

One campaign in personal evangelism cannot set your church into an eternal orbit of soul winning. But it can do something mass evangelism cannot do. It *can* sustain soul winning for several months.

BUT!!

Have a *second* soul winning campaign in your church, and you can start expecting the *impossible* to happen. More people will participate in the second campaign. There will be even greater interest. The second time, more of your people know what to expect, and what to plan for.

There will be greater results, too. And from the second campaign, you can expect a large number of your people to arrive at a new plateau of witnessing. Many will begin witnessing everywhere they go, and every day. This is the ultimate end of evangelism: evangelism that is a natural, daily part of the layman's life. You will soon notice that you have a nucleus of soul winners who just will not quit. As one pastor put it, "They wouldn't stop winning souls if I started preaching against it."

If you were to make a graph of a campaign in *mass* evangelism, indicating the sustaining quality of its evangelistic results, the graph line would drop to zero as soon as the meeting ended. A graph on *personal* evangelism would go straight out for a long time, and then begin to slowly drop. *But* after two or three Campaigns in personal evangelism, instead of dropping, the graph would continue to travel in a straight line. There would be no dropping. This would indicate you had to come to a point of *sustained evangelism*. Regardless of what does or does not happen in your church then, you have a nucleus of people who will continue to win souls, come what may. *This is Sustained Evangelism!*

You see, personal evangelism can do a remarkable thing: unlike mass evangelism, the more you repeat it, the stronger and more effective it becomes. Until at last it becomes the magnificent obsession of laymen.

Your church can have SUSTAINED evangelism!

It is arrived at by *repeated training*.

II. THE PASTOR'S PART IN SUSTAINED EVANGELISM

1. Continue to win souls yourself.

   If ever you stop winning souls, once you have begun, your people will know it. Keep it up.

2. Let your people know you are winning souls.

   This is not to make a show of it, but to constantly remind your people that this has become the theme of your life. You can use illustrations in your sermons, about people you have talked to, people you have won. A soul winning interview can illustrate almost any point you'll ever speak on. There are many other ways to remind your people you are still at the job.

3. Use the Announcement Period.

   A pastor can increase his effectiveness as a leader, by simply *planning* his announcement period. Announcements can be both entertaining and informative.

   Every time you make announcements, mention soul winning! Announce visitation. Why? Your church must see that it has shifted directions; that it is sailing a charted course; that whatever else comes and goes from week to week, there is *one* underlying emphasis that will remain.

III.

THE PASTOR MUST GIVE CREDIT TO SOUL WINNERS

1. When a few of your people first begin making efforts to witness, mention it in some of your messages.

2. Here is a real key: when you introduce new Christians as they come into the fellowship of the church, also give recognition to the one who won him to Christ. If your church has an "invitation" to receive people into the church membership, then have the new Christian to stand, and call on the soul winner who won him to come and stand with his convert.

3. The author wishes every church would be informal enough to do this next suggestion. It would *keep* revival going in your church.

When a new convert comes into your church (say, at the close of the service), have him give his testimony. Then have the layman who won him stand and tell about the conversion. Then take a moment to remind your people of why this has happened. "It happened because we have people going out every (Thursday) visiting in homes and talking to men about Christ. Everyone in this church should be here for Evangelism Day."

Plug your visitation program!

The author recalls one church that missed a great blessing. This church had a two-week campaign, with a week of intensive visiting. It was a little church that had never seen many conversions, though it was in an ideal location, in a city of one million people.

That Sunday morning, following the week of visiting, the pastor gave the invitation. It lasted only about five seconds. Everyone seemed to be on their feet moving. Sixteen came forward instantly. All had found Christ in their homes that week. (Fourteen more came that evening.) The pastor took the names of those who responded to the invitation, read the names of his congregation and dismissed the service!

Had he taken only a moment more, that church could have experienced a Pentecost. One convert was a Jew (won to Christ by a man who had never witnessed before). There was a young couple with a wonderful conversion experience. Another family had been re-united in Christ.

The pastor could have called on these people to give their testimonies, or he could have at least told the story for them. He could have asked the Christians who won them to come and stand with their converts and tell the story. He missed an opportunity to simply disclose the riches of glory in Christ Jesus.

Defrost your Sunday services and "straight jacket" ritual. If you believe in the power of God, start letting it be demonstrated. Give the Holy Spirit a chance . . . and "let the redeemed of the Lord say so"!

4. Give credit to all who visit.

When someone comes to make a public profession of faith in Christ, ask this question: "How many of you have ever visited in the home of Mr.................?" Ask for a show of hands.

"How many of you have ever prayed for him?"

Then observe, "All of you have a part in his conversion."

This encourages everyone who is trying to witness.

IV. HAVE A TIME OF TESTIMONIES

Either on Sunday evening or Wednesday evening each week, have a time of testimony. When a church becomes a "doer of the Word, and not a hearer only", then there is a great deal that is new to testify about. Most churches stopped having testimonial time because there was nothing to testify about! There is now!

Give everyone an opportunity to testify of their experience in visitation and in "extra-curricular" witnessing. This is also a good time to present prayer requests for those still being witnessed to.

This testimonial time can be a season of rejoicing and prayer. It can also set off a real desire in the hearts of others who are still sitting on the sidelines, to get into visitation.

Let your people hear — and tell — what great things God is doing.

V. CALL FOR COMMITMENTS

Every week, for at least two months, have a specific time, (on Sunday or Wednesday), when you call on Christians to commit themselves to visit.

Let's say it is Sunday evening and testimonial time is over. Ask everyone who is going visiting *next* week to *hold up their hands*. This is one of the most important keys to sustained evangelism. This forces everyone to publicly decide they will or will not attempt to be a witness. It also serves to show those who are not visiting, just how few, until now, are carrying the load of soul winning.

This also serves to spotlight the fact that you really mean business — that you *expect* them to witness. Each week you will notice that a few more hands go up! By keeping this weekly commitment up, you can grow a truly tremendous visitation group.

VI. TAKE A NEW APPROACH TO RECOGNIZING SUNDAY VISITORS

Perhaps you have never thought about this, but you have only ONE source in the world for church growth — for any kind of additions whatever to your church.
Your only source of growth is visitors to your church. Before a man can ever be a member of your church, he first has to be a *visitor* to your church.

Visitors are usually neglected.

Now, most churches think they are *very* friendly. They are, too, — to one another. Not to visitors, though. Laymen are afraid to go up to a perfect stranger in the church and introduce themselves. (They are afraid the "stranger", may turn out to be one of the deacons!)

Most churches ask visitors to fill out a visitor's card. But even then, a visitor can go away never really feeling welcomed, and often never even receiving a single handshake. You need a system whereby *every* visitor will be recognized, *and* warmly welcomed by the church.

This is easy to do.

When it is time to recognize visitors, simply ask all the members of the church to stand, and all the visitors to remain seated. This makes it easy to spot visitors, and it prevents them from having to stand to be recognized. Then ask the Christians to introduce themselves and shake hands with those visitors who are seated nearby. Then ask all those who are seated to fill out a visitors card. Every visitor is greeted and identified this way.

Like it or not, the greatest single factor that determines where people move their membership is this: *how friendly is the church?*

VII. HAVE SPECIAL EMPHASIS ON SOUL WINNING THROUGHOUT THE YEAR

Every few months you should have an emphasis in your church that spotlights certain areas of soul winning. Listed here are a few. Be sure to place them on your "Calendar of Evangelism".

1. A drive to get everyone to carry a New Testament.

No one can be a soul winner, no matter how gifted, if he doesn't have a Testament to witness with. Put on a drive to have every man and woman in your church to carry a Testament. Get your people to show one another they are carrying their Testaments, when they meet throughout the week.

This will not only solve the need of Christians carrying the New Testament at all times, but it can also be a great deal of fun centered around the idea of soul winning.

It can make everyone more conscious of the need of being a consistent witness.

2. Put on a drive for everyone to carry tracts.

Make up several hundred "tract packets" — one for every adult member of your church. Put on a drive to get Christians to carry these packets: (1) in their cars, to give to service station attendants; (2) to keep them in the office desk, or factory locker, etc.; and (3) for ladies, in their purses, and men in their billfold or in the New Testament they are supposed to be carrying at all times!

3. Have a drive for every home to put up a Tract Rack.

A tract rack is a little wooden (or metal or plastic) rack, nailed up somewhere near the front door, filled with evangelistic tracts. Every Christian home should be challenged to have one. Every person who knocks on the door should be given a tract.

Here, again, is a chance to focus attention on the opportunity of daily witnessing for Christ.

4. Have a SOUL WINNING RETREAT FOR YOUR MEN.

Rent out a lodge, and have a retreat for your men. Begin it on Friday night, have it to last all day Saturday. Return to the church on Sunday. Plan a special visitation emphasis for your men the following week.

Here's how to schedule the meeting: On Friday evening, speak on the subject of "Walking in the power of the Spirit", or some other emphasis on the deeper spiritual life that gives power to witness.

Take all day Saturday to do nothing but train the laymen in soul winning. (Eight hours of soul winning training all in one "lump" is better than only one hour for six nights.) This can be a spiritual and physical treat for your men. Challenge them anew to soul winning in the weeks to come.

(The author has conducted such retreats across America and has found them to be the best way of all to lead Christians to be soul winners.)

VIII. MAKE THE SUNDAY SCHOOL A GREAT SOUL WINNING INSTITUTION.

(100,000 lost people could be easily won to Christ *next Sunday* if the following suggestions were to be carried out in every evangelistically minded church in America.)

There is no easier or more ideal place in the world to win a soul to Christ than (1) in an empty Sunday School classroom, (2) right after Sunday School, (3) when it is only ten minutes before worship service, (4) witnessing to someone who is obviously interested.

All a Christian has to do is step up to a visitor, just as the Sunday School class is over, and begin talking to him. The rest of the class will be leaving. In a moment, the classroom will be empty. Find out if the visitor knows Christ. If he doesn't, win him.

IF YOU, THE PASTOR, WILL TRAIN YOUR PEOPLE TO START DOING THIS SIMPLE ACT OF WITNESSING RIGHT AFTER SUNDAY SCHOOL EACH WEEK, YOUR CHURCH CAN WIN THREE TIMES AS MANY PEOPLE TO CHRIST AS IT IS NOW . . . EVEN IF YOU *NEVER* HAVE A VISITATION PROGRAM.

IX. ESTABLISH A PERMANENT CLASS IN SOUL WINNING TRAINING

In another place in this book, it was pointed out that one of the few things that the nation's most evangelistic churches have in common, is that all have a year-round program of soul winning *training*.

You can run a Sunday evening class on soul winning for six to ten weeks. Bring all your new converts into the class. (They make the best of soul winners.) Keep plugging the class, getting those who are not active in the visitation program to begin this training program.

Repeat the class continually. Many will want a refresher course too.

Also, establish a section of books in your church library if you have one, on the best soul winning methods. Encourage your people to study the books.

X. DEVELOP NEW SOUL WINNERS

Developing new soul winners is one of the most gratifying experiences in life. As you notice a Christian who is showing an interest in witnessing, do all you can to encourage him. Be sure he is trained properly. On Visitation Day, send him out with the best, most effective soul winners. At the end of the visitation hour, take special care to talk with him and encourage him.

Here is the greatest secret of all: when you discover someone who will be really easy to win to Christ, don't win that person yourself. Get someone to do it who has just started trying to win souls.

On each Evangelism Day, the pastor should pick some new person to take with him visiting. Develop him. Spend time with him. Write him a letter of encouragement. Remember that when you have developed a soul winner, you have doubled the effectiveness of your own Christian life.

XI. DEMAND EVANGELISM FROM YOUR STAFF AND CHURCH LEADERS

There should be a *hard core* of people witnessing and winning people to Christ, regardless of the state of repairs your visitation program is in. Demand of your staff that they each spend *one day per week* knocking on doors.

Do the same thing with your teachers and deacons. Demand that they visit each week. If you can't get some of your teachers to witness, then you should revert to a New Testament principle: less quantity and more quality. Fewer teachers, but more quality in teaching. Ultimately, it always reaps more results!

Also keep in mind that you yourself should have a certain time for witnessing. This is the key to every great soul winner's life. At least one day a week you must give to winning the lost.

XII. CONTINUE TO EMPHASIZE THE
S P I R I T   FILLED LIFE

We cannot make too much of this point. Continue to teach and preach and emphasize the Spirit Filled Life. It is not only essential to a fruitful life, but it is the key to abundant living. Your people need, and must have this, to be soul winners. With it, you will have more than a soul winning church! You will have a deeply spiritual church!

There comes a time of breakthrough in all this. It is a time when "everyone in the city seems to become a prospect". Suddenly, prospects are everywhere, and the whole city takes note that something has happened in your church.

If you live among the people in your community, in their homes, and dare to reach out to them, even in such places as taverns, they will respect you for it. They will look toward you with trust. They will even begin making themselves available to the church for spiritual help.

The whole climate about you will begin to take on a New Testament atmosphere. Christians will begin to expect God to do great things in every realm of their lives, their community, and their church. There can even come a time when the Christians will *expect* to see souls being won to Christ every week of the year, and will be willing to lay their own lives on the altar to achieve this as a reality for their church, 52 weeks a year.

CHAPTER 25

A PROGRAM OF FOLLOW UP
FOR EVANGELISTIC CHURCHES

A pastor once asked me to address his board of deacons on the need of starting a church program of follow up. I began something like this:

"A church needs at least a ten-week course of study to introduce the new convert to the Christian life. The convert needs to learn exactly how to pray; he needs to be introduced to the Bible and how to study it; he needs to learn God's method for raising children, for getting along with husband or wife; he needs to know how to be completely victorious over the problems of worry, persecution, despondency, and how to deal with the problem of sin . . . "

A deacon interrupted me, saying, "The new Christian isn't the only one who needs all that. I've been a Christian for 15 years, a deacon for ten; and I've never been taught any of this!"

What is the greatest single need of the church today?

Perhaps it is this: A dynamic follow up on new converts.

We could stop the cycle of "low quality" Christians, by growing a generation of victorious new converts.

At this writing, the author does not know of a single denomination in America that has a program designed to introduce the new convert into the Christian life. The average new Christian today is simply dropped into a Sunday School class — if he shows up for Sunday School the week after his conversion. (If not, we have no plan for reaching him in the home.) There he sits in Sunday School beside a man who may have been a Christian for 30 years. Both study the same lesson! If it happens to be the book of Obadiah . . . that's what he studies, for his first Bible lesson!

WHY THE NEGLECT?

One reason *follow up* has been neglected is because mass evangelism and enlistment evangelism have not focused attention on its need. In both mass and enlistment evangelism, the convert always comes to Christ *inside* the church building. He is already attending church and can be brought immediately into church fellowship. He can be taken into the Sunday School, and all the other church organizations.

The need of *follow up* has always been eminent, but personal evangelism focuses attention on this need. When a man is won to Christ in the home, he is a long way from the church building. Immediately everyone will begin to sense the need of a program of follow up to help this new "babe in Christ" grow strong in the Lord.

A program to develop the new Christian is one of the greatest needs of the 20th century church. This chapter can only highlight the need. It will rest with another — you, the pastor — to create that program.

Follow up falls into two categories: follow up at the moment of decision; and follow up by introducing the convert to the Christian life.

I.

FOLLOW UP INSIDE THE CHURCH

The Need of Follow Up at the Point of Decision

There are three ways most churches win people to Christ, inside the church building.

(1) The open invitation, when the unconverted are invited to walk down the aisle and the pastor receives them.

(2) The counsel room, where the "seeker" goes to talk with the pastor or some other Christian.

(3) The altar call, where the lost are invited to kneel "to be prayed for".

What happens after the "seeker" comes forward?

In the Open Invitation:

The pastor has preached a message. At the close he issues an invitation to all who would receive Christ to "come". The music begins, and someone starts down the aisle.

For some reason, we seem to assume that the person coming forward is converted by the time he takes the pastor by the hand. While the music continues in their ears, the pastor will usually ask, "Do you want to receive Christ as Saviour? And be baptized? And become a member of this church? Do you believe in Jesus Christ as your Saviour?"

After a perfunctory "yes" to all these questions, the individual is asked to "sit down here and fill out this card".

That's not conversion!

We are literally bringing millions of people into our churches this way. A gigantic host of them are *still lost* when they are received into the church's fellowship.

This is especially true of a child. You can ask a child, "Do you believe in Jesus Christ, and do you want to accept Him as your Saviour," and you will always get a "yes" answer. There are no six-year-old or ten-year-old atheists! You could also ask him, "Do you believe in Santa Claus and the Easter Bunny", and you would still get a "yes" answer.

Every person who comes forward, regardless of his age, needs someone to read one or two Scriptures explaining exactly and clearly how to receive Christ as his Saviour. Then he, himself, should turn to Christ and personally call on Christ to save him.

In The Counsel Room:

We are making essentially the same mistakes in the counsel room. The questions are sometimes a little more theological, but no closer to the real need: the need of an individual to personally encounter Christ in an experience of salvation.

At the Altar:

The procedure at the altar is just as critical. The seeker will kneel at the altar. Traditionally, a group of Christians gather around him and begin praying for him. The author has watched that process continue for upwards of an hour . . . yet with not one person ever slipping up to the "seeker" to open a Bible and explain *how* to receive Christ. Often, no effort is made to personally lead the man to Christ.

What happens as a result of our failure to lead men through the experience of conversion?

We have populated our churches with unconverted people! They come sincerely responding to the Gospel message. Knowing nothing themselves, they place themselves at our disposal. If we tell them to fill out a card, that is what they do. If they answer a few obvious questions with a "yes", and we begin treating them as though they were Christians, they assume they are.

It is not the fault of the church member that he is lost. It is our fault, in failing at the most critical point of all!

Pastors often say, "One-third to one-half of my membership is totally inactive". Many pastors believe that perhaps half of the membership of their churches are *lost*.

This terrible situation need not exist. We can stop it right now! All we need is a counseling program that gets down to cases.

How to win those who come:

The solution to this grave problem is very simple. The pastor should train a small group of laymen and women to assist him in "drawing the net" of conversion.

The pastor or layman should thoroughly explain the plan of salvation and show the person coming forward, exactly how to receive Christ. The person seeking eternal life should be shown exactly how to call on Christ to come into his life as Lord and Saviour, and then be led to do so. Carry him into, and through the experience of calling on Christ.

Special emphasis and care needs to be taken with children.

Regardless of how your church receives converts, by invitation, counsel room, or altar — follow up can be done so very simply.

———

One other word needs to be added here. A Baptist pastor in Georgia started a counseling program for *church members* who came forward to transfer their membership to his church. He personally counseled with each person, . . . in his study after service. Here is what he told the author he had discovered:

"At least half of all church members who move their membership are not coming because of *church loyalty*. They are coming because of a great spiritual *upheaval* in their own lives. In desperation, not knowing what else to do, they transfer their church membership."

He went on to say that nearly half of those who come moving their membership are unconverted. He easily wins them to Christ in his study after only a moment of counsel and questioning.

He also observed that several "Baptists" were not Baptists at all, but just thought they were. They were neither Christians, nor had they ever been baptized, nor were they in any way members of a sister church.

Lastly, he noted that people who come to change

their affiliation from some other denomination need the greatest attention. Most come because of marriage, or some similar factor which makes a change of denominations expedient. In other words, they are not joining the church for any *spiritual* reason. He observed that in his experience, the vast majority of these people are completely unconverted. Of course, in that personal interview, the pastor easily leads them to an experience of salvation.

So a program of counseling those who *transfer* church membership also needs to be created.

A PROGRAM TO INTRODUCE
THE NEW CONVERT TO THE CHRISTIAN LIFE:

The second stage of follow up comes in instructing the convert in the Christian venture. He can be spared years of spiritual floundering, and perhaps be saved from the fate of becoming an "inactive member", by a few weeks of orientation into a spiritual life in Christ.

Few churches have any program for growing "babes in Christ". Some have a "New Members Class". This is for *all* who enter the church membership, whether as a new Christian, or by transfer of membership. This is usually a four or eight week class on subjects such as, "What it Means to be a Christian", "Our Church Organization", "Our Denominational Distinctives", "Our Mission Program", "Being a Good Steward".

A new Christian can go through this class, and still not have the vaguest notion of how to live a victorious Christian life. This is just like trying to teach your one-day-old baby all about the family finances!

SETTING UP A CLASS FOR NEW CHRISTIANS

The new converts class should be taught on Sunday morning, at the regular Sunday School hour. (A new convert is not ready to go into a regular Sunday School class, for he has no concept of the material being covered.)

Here is a list of ten sessions and what to cover. Because virtually nothing has ever been done on this subject, you will have to create the material. Let us hope the day will come when a curriculum of study for new Christians will be created.

1. The Christian Adventure
   (An introduction to the Christian Life.)

2. The Abundant Life
   (How to live victoriously)

3. Meet the Bible
   (Tell the entire story of the Bible in 45 min.)

4. How to Study the Bible
   (Give a practice plan, then make an assignment, so that each person can try the plan, and report the results next week.)

5. How to Study the Bible (continued)
   (Go over the results of last week's effort.)

6. How to Pray
   (A simple step-by-step plan)

7. The Christian Home
   (Duties of husband, wife, children; how to have family prayer)

8. How to Witness to Others
   (Present an effective soul winning plan)

9. The Christian and Stewardship
   (Stewardship of time, talent, material wealth)

10. The Christian and the Holy Spirit.
    (Emphasis on the Spirit filled life.)

There may be others, such as: obedience; how to know God's will; or some directed studies, etc. There should be one last session with the new convert. It should be an introductory lesson, explaining the book of the Bible that is being *studied* in the *regular* Sunday School classes. He can then transfer into a Sunday School with a good background on the material being covered in the lessons.

I am personally convinced that a new Christian needs to go through two years of special training before going into a regular Sunday School class. I also realize that this is too radical an idea for most churches, therefore, I have suggested 10 weeks.

II.

FOLLOW UP OUTSIDE THE CHURCH

There is a second area of follow up. It has always been neglected. When a church starts winning souls, it becomes critical! It is:

FOLLOW UP ON CONVERTS WHO DO NOT COME TO CHURCH

What can be done for people who make a decision in their home, but who "never come to church"? Is there a solution?

The loss of converts won through personal evangelism bothers churches more than the loss of converts won in mass evangelism. Recently a church had over *100* people to come forward in a mass evangelism campaign. But at the end of the year, only *50* people were added to the church during the whole 12-month period! This kind of statistics is rarely ever mentioned. Because of the *impersonal* nature of mass evangelism, the losses are not noticed as much.

In personal evangelism, every person who does not unite with the church stands out as a glaring problem. This author is convinced that far more people who are won to Christ in the homes unite with a church, than do those won through any other avenues of evangelism.

Nonetheless, some don't. Why? What can be done about it?

WHY DO SOME NOT UNITE WITH THE CHURCH?

Let's look at it from the lost man's viewpoint:

The lost man has not been to church in years. He gets up every morning of his life and goes to work in a mad rush. At the job, he curses and tells vulgar jokes. He blames the government for everything. He doesn't like his boss. He smokes, he drinks, he's got a bad temper. On the way home, he stops at the tavern for a beer. When he gets home he's cross. He yells at the kids. He and his wife have a violent argument. He sits down to the evening paper, then turns on the TV and watches it until he falls to sleep.

This is his life!

What about his wife?

She gets up in the morning, perhaps spends a large part of it fussing with the children. She wears shorts all day ... gossips with the neighbors ... reads *True Confessions*, then *watches* the same things on TV, while playing jazz on the radio. The rest of the day, she spends talking with a friend about the latest Hollywood scandal. She is shallow, immature, selfish, and self centered. She is hot tempered, too.

The children are all spoiled.

This is the typical home of an American family who do not know Christ as their Saviour. All the pressure and influence that surrounds them 24 hours a day are *materialistic* and *godless*.

Then one night, while they are all sitting around watching TV, there is a knock at the door. Two Christians have come to visit. In a few minutes, they are talking about Jesus Christ. Immediately the lost husband senses his need, and realizes this is the answer to his meaningless life. He accepts Christ as his Saviour. The Christians invite him to their church, and leave.

The next day, his wife is still self-centered, immature and high tempered. As he gets in the car with his friends, they still curse and drink and talk vulgarly. He goes back into a life that still subjects him to the same godless grind for 24 hours a day. This has been his life for 30 years. He has had only 45 minutes of influence from the opposite direction. That's all!

And we expect that man to come, on his own steam, to a strange church (filled with strange people) and join it the very next Sunday!

We are expecting too much!

It is a tribute to the power of the Gospel that as many come as do.

For many people, who have almost no spiritual background, there is a tremendous gap which exists between the *moment* they receive Christ in the home, and the time when they are spiritually *capable* of joining a church.

Whoever gave us the idea that we were supposed to expect every convert to automatically join a church after conversion? That is a huge step for many people. For one thing, if nothing else, there are many people who are frightened to death at the thought of having to "go down there and join". This is a very frightening thought for people who have no religious background, especially.

This is another fact pastors often overlook.

Most people who are won to Christ in mass evangelism and enlistment evangelism *do* have a spiritual background. If they didn't, they probably would not be coming to church. But in personal evangelism you go to the masses and you run into a new world of people — people who have *no* religious background whatsoever. They will need your special help. They do not conform to traditional patterns that we have set up.

Some new converts must be *built up to the level of joining a church.* That can be done only by *follow up* in the *home!*

A PROGRAM OF FOLLOW UP IN THE HOME

Most converts won to Christ in the home will unite with a church after three or four Bible classes in their own home. This is a new concept for most pastors today. It is very New Testament, though. Almost all Christian fellowship was centered in the home in the first century.

Here is what the pastor can do: Train a small number of men and women (about four to eight people will usually do) to make follow up visits in the homes of the converts.

The Christian should telephone the convert, explain the purpose of the call, and then ask for an appointment to "come by and talk awhile and study some Scriptures together". The layman can except to get almost 100 per cent cooperation from every new Christian he calls. (After all, the new convert does not know this is unusual!)

The Christian should then go to the home and begin teaching the "New Christian's Class" to the convert right there in his home. Have one session each week. After a few weeks, the two will become friends. The new convert will begin growing, and losing his fear. He will develop an honest, sincere desire for church and Christian fellowship. It becomes a very simple task to bring the convert into the church.

This idea of follow up in the home may be new to you. But it is a powerful idea. It not only rescues the new Christian, but also grows the Christian who does the teaching.

For one pastor in Colorado, this plan worked so perfectly that he began using it on all his inactive members. This was his report: "We have reclaimed every family in our church that has allowed us to have as many as four study sessions in the home!"

Here, again, is the simple answer; taking Christ into the homes, not only in soul winning but also in follow up!

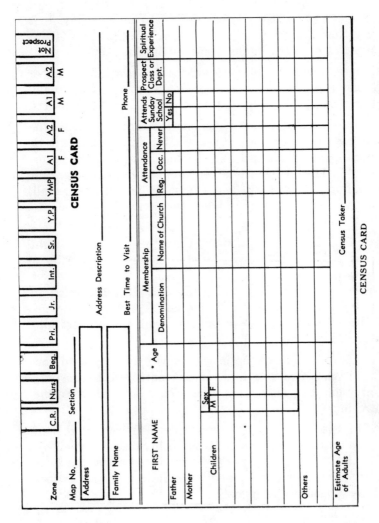

CENSUS CARD

Card No. 7-5330, size 7" x 5", may be obtained from Gospel Publishing House, Springfield, Missouri 65802

248

VISITATION REPORT Family Name _____

Address _____

1st. Visit Date _____ Visitor(s) _____
Not at home _____

Comments _____

2nd. Visit Date _____ Visitor(s) _____
Not at home _____

Comments _____

3rd. Visit Date _____ Visitor(s) _____
Not at home _____

Comments _____

4th. Visit Date _____ Visitor(s) _____
Not at home _____

Comments _____

5th. Visit Date _____ Visitor(s) _____
Not at home _____

Comments _____

Instructions

Coding: Card is coded on reverse side for tabbing by age level. Key to adult coding: A-1—ages 25-40; A-2 —above 40; F—female; M—male.
Census-taker should not fill out card in family's presence. Regardless of church membership, find out if family has had salvation experience.
Card should be returned to church after each use in visitation.

Family moved from _____ to _____

Form 7-5330   Gospel Publishing House, Springfield, Mo.   Printed in U.S.A.

CENSUS CARD

Reverse side

NOTES

NOTES

NOTES

NOTES

NOTES

NOTES

NOTES